W9-BIP-339

WHY QUITTERS WIN

Decide to be Excellent

By Nick Tasler

LEADERS IN GLOBAL PUBLISHING

Contents

INTRODUCTION

THE CURIOUS CASE OF THE YELLOWSTONE FIRE

"When you come to a fork in the road, take it."

--Yogi Berra

On an overcast day in the middle of June 1988, Jim Barrett and two friends were driving up Daisy Pass on the northern edge of Yellowstone National Park when they spotted something. Off in the distance to their left, they saw two figures meandering aimlessly through a grassy, tree-lined meadow. As the pair got closer, Barrett realized that they were a man and his dog clad in "scorched clothing and fur." Jim Barrett slowed his car to ask if the man was okay. When the stranger and his companion reached the vehicle, Barrett remembers thinking that the duo smelled like they had just rolled around in a campfire. He also noticed that the man needed first aid. Fast. Barrett and his friends tucked the strangers into the car and drove back down Daisy Pass into their hometown of Cooke City, Montana.

Along the way, the man explained that he had been camping at Yellowstone when he and his dog were completely overtaken by a raging fire they hadn't seen coming. With no other choice, the man hurried his dog to a nearby creek and leaped in. When the flames roared overhead, he held his dog under his arm beneath the surface of the frigid, mountain-fed spring until the blaze passed.

With their camping supplies smoldering under a pile of ashes, they spent the night huddled together under a tree until the next morning, when they could finally begin hiking again. It was at that point when Barrett spotted them. Neither Barrett and his friends nor the stranger could have known then, but by the end of August, the Storm Creek Fire would join over 250 other fires. Collectively, the firestorm would end up transforming more than 1.5 million acres of America's first National Park into a blazing inferno. It would cause public outrage from the Pacific Northwest all the way to the steps of Capitol Hill.

But the Yellowstone Fires of 1988 also did something else. They illustrated one of the most profound yet widely misunderstood lessons about the nature of excellence and the decisions that make excellence possible.

1. Let it Burn

The summer of 1988 began peacefully at Yellowstone National Park. Just like every summer before it for almost a century since Yellowstone became a national park, thousands of visitors each day flocked to the real-world home of Yogi Bear. Hoping for a brief escape from the fast-paced hustle of the daily grind, recreational campers, family vacationers, and nature-lovers all sought to lose themselves in the majestic pine trees. They wanted to breathe in the fresh mountain air and to catch an up-close glimpse of a bear, or maybe a wolf or an elk. Some would spend their days hiking through the woods, while others set out to try their luck with a fishing pole and a tackle box, while still others marveled at the wonder of the Old Faithful geyser. These were the things that Yellowstone National Park was all about in the summer months. Perhaps that explains part of the reason why the Storm Creek Fire that Jim Barrett had witnessed was conspicuously absent from June's Daily Park Briefings for the Yellowstone ranger staff.

Instead, June's briefing focused almost entirely on rather commonplace happenings such as bear sightings near camping trails, or on national news like the drought that was sweeping the nation. When lightning struck a lodgepole pine tree on the southwest edge of the Park and sparked another small fire a little more than a week after the Storm Creek Fire began in the north, the event went largely unnoticed by the park's rangers.

Finally, on the first day of July, the Yellowstone Daily Briefing noted that another fire was triggered near the pristine shores of Lake Lewis. Over 2,000 miles away in Washington D.C., National Parks Director William Mott received notice of what was happening at Yellowstone. Mott did nothing. He issued no order to extinguish the fires. Minute after minute, day by day, the flames crept through the forest, swallowing one tree after the next. Two weeks later, an approaching fire forced Vice President of the United States George H.W. Bush to cut short a backcountry fishing trip on the eastern edge of the Park. It wasn't until the week following the Vice President's return that Mott finally began ordering fire crews to contain the blaze. By then, however, it seemed to be too late. In spite of the valiant efforts of thousands of firefighters on the ground, in addition to helicopters and airplanes dousing the Park with water from the skies, the fire's intensity only grew. On August

20, a day now referred to as "Black Saturday," flames climbed more than 200 feet in the air and consumed over 150,000 acres of forest. More of Yellowstone National Park turned to ash on Black Saturday alone than the previous 100 years of wildfires combined. *The Washington Post* compared the carnage and chaos of Black Saturday to the attack on the U.S. air base in Da Nang, Vietnam.

The question that an outraged public, a skeptical Congress, and a critical media wanted answered was *why didn't the Park Service stop it?* More specifically, *why didn't Bill Mott stop it?* Was Mott simply a pawn for a Reagan Administration whom Mott's predecessor at the National Park System claimed "had the most obscene environmental record in history?" Or was the incident just another piece of evidence pointing to the ineptitude of government agencies—a tragic foreshadowing of the bungled government response to Hurricane Katrina two decades later? Or perhaps Bill Mott was just another career bureaucrat who had failed his way up into a leadership position and was destined to defy common sense when his nation needed him most?

While each question hinted at a plausible explanation, in fact, none was correct. There was another reason behind Bill Mott's curious behavior that almost nobody considered. The real reason was so counterintuitive that it seemed patently absurd and illogical to the majority of people. The fact of the matter is too strange to be fiction: Extinguishing forest fires is an enormous fire hazard. That's why Bill Mott adhered to a strict "let it burn" policy for forest fires within national parks.

2. The Paradox of Quitting

The late Bill Mott had a trim build with square shoulders and a white tuft of thinning hair. After declining President Nixon's request to take command of the National Park Service in 1969, William Mott somewhat reluctantly agreed to take the post when it was offered to him again in 1985 by Ronald Reagan. By 1988, his distinguished career had made Mott the only 3-time winner of the Pugsley Medal, which honors the outstanding efforts of Americans who champion the cause of parks and conservation. Although nearing his 80th birthday, William Mott's wrinkled blue eyes and contagious smile still exuded the vigor that characterized his five decades of civil service. Mott had earned a reputation for being both a visionary and a pragmatic man of action with a relentless passion for protecting and expanding public spaces. During the last three decades of his life, it was generally accepted that if you cared at all about your public parks, Bill Mott was the guy you wanted taking care of them. It was that reputation that made his response to the Yellowstone Fires all the more puzzling. The confusion was widespread and included just about everyone—everyone, that is, except for a handful of experienced, well-informed naturalists and ecologists.

Think about the last time you've either visited, driven by on the highway, or saw one of America's national forests on TV. Chances are, you found lush vegetation and a beautifully dense blanket of green cloaking the scene. That is due almost entirely to the efforts of the federal government. Ever since the mid 1940's, a series of

Public Service Announcements starring the U.S. Forest Service's (not to be confused with the National Park Service) most famous employee, Smokey Bear, urged Americans to prevent forest fires. By the time of the Yellowstone Fires four decades after Smokey's debut, the message had stuck. Virtually every American, including representatives in congress and broadcast journalists, agreed that fires are a destructive force. From there, the logic went like this: Trees are good. Fire burns trees. Ergo, fire is bad. The line of reasoning was simple, perhaps deceptively so.

In the 1960's, ecologists who made their living studying forests began challenging the wildfires-are-evil argument. What the ecologists knew that few other people did is that wildfires are essential to the health of a forest. Forest fires are like nature's way of gardening. Seedling trees are able to establish themselves after fire clears out the underbrush and returns nutrients back into the soil. Possibly the strangest and certainly the most counterintuitive benefit of wildfires is that small fires are necessary for preventing big fires. It works like this: Periodically, lightning will strike a tree in a forest. Flames grow. The fires burn some but not all of the vegetation, and then eventually die out. In the case of lodgepole pines, seeds actually require the intense heat of a fire to germinate. For millions of years, this cycle of burning has taken place. Early European settlers and ancient Native Americans knew that putting out fires not only deteriorates the health of a forest, it also significantly increases the risk of unnaturally large and ultimately uncontrollable fires that frequently ravage nearby homes and businesses—precisely the kinds of fires that are sparking with increasing frequency today throughout the western United States.

When those natural fires are extinguished by human intervention, the grasses, saplings, and shrubs create what ecologists call a "fuel ladder". Imagine a very long ladder that starts on the ground and extends to the top of the tallest trees. Like any ladder, the ladder's purpose is to help its climber climb higher, only the climber of a fuel ladder is not a person; it is a flame. Rung by rung, a fire that ignites on the ground can climb up the smaller brush until it reaches the highest trees. When the tallest trees start to burn, the entire forest as well as the surrounding homes and businesses are in danger. But ever since 1908, the policy of the U.S. Forest Service (again, not the same as the Park Service) has been to attack all wildfires with severe prejudice. As a result, the lush forests we admire are now crawling with fuel ladders. As author and UCLA scientist, Jared Diamond writes in his book *Collapse*, after the 1980's "people began to realize that the U.S. Federal Government's fire suppression policy was contributing to those big fires, and that natural fires caused by lightning had previously played an important role in maintaining forest structure." It was that body of evidence that inspired the National Park Service's leaders back in 1968 to make a decision. In order to insure that America's national parks continued to thrive, and in order to protect the people and the homes and the businesses near those parks, the National Park Service decided to *quit* fighting fires.

It turns out that Bill Mott's failure to extinguish the Yellowstone Fires of 1988 was no failure at all.

I think our organizations, our careers, and our lives are a lot like forests. In the spirit of full disclosure, I am not an ecologist or a naturalist. In fact, the only times I've voluntarily "camped" in my adult life I've been within arm's length of a central air conditioning unit, a full kitchen, and a flat screen TV inside of a 31-foot motorhome. Regardless of your camping prowess or nascent interest in forestry, people like you and me can learn something very important about the power of strategic quitting from wrapping our minds around the curious relationship between forests and wildfires.

3. From Mediocrity to Excellence

At its heart, this book is about the counterintuitive idea that quitting is vital to the pursuit of excellence. Many talented teams and highly competent individuals find themselves trapped on a plateau of mediocrity because they can't decide what *not* to do.

In the following pages, I want to do two things for you. First, I want to convince you that producing volume is not the same as pursuing excellence. Doing *more* is not the same as doing *better*. The pursuit of excellence requires some projects to be swallowed by flames. Some opportunities need to go up in smoke. Some options need to be rejected. Sometimes, nature will start the fire for you, but most times you must strike the match with a conscious decision. We will meet a group of people who have tapped into the power of quitting to outperform their better educated and more privileged peers. We will meet a practitioner-scholar whose research reveals why the combination of thinking strategically and acting decisively amounts to what is almost a super power that saved Apple Computer and elevated Starbucks back to prominence. In these and other examples, you'll see that quitters win because they pursue excellence with decisive focus, not scattered productivity.

Second, I want to provide you with an elegantly simple 3-part framework for putting this idea into practice with every decision you make, every day. You will discover what a Decision Pulse is and how to use your Team Pulse to provide a new level of clarity for your team. I will present a surprisingly simple way to improve the quality of your decisions without getting lost in a jungle of data or becoming paralyzed by the fear of making the wrong choice. In the real world, the pursuit of excellence does not happen with a single decision at an annual retreat. It is not a quarterly event or even a monthly meeting. Every organization, every team, and every person must pursue excellence one decision at a time, multiple times every day. In the final chapters, you will learn how you and the people on your team can leverage the forces of process, personality, and pressure to pursue excellence every day both personally and professionally.

Why Quitters Win is not a book for everyone. If your deadbeat cousin has never held onto a job or a mate for longer than a month, then an inability to quit is not his biggest obstacle to excellence. Similarly, if you are content with mediocrity in your work and a mundane existence for your life, then this book is probably not for you, either. On the other hand, if you are inspired by the pursuit of excellence in your work, in your community, or in your home and you are ready to make an impact on your world that outlasts your time in it, then I encourage you to read on. The rest of this book will challenge you. At times, it will even make you uncomfortable. And that's a good thing. It means the message is sinking in.

But the rest of this book will also excite you. For you, this book might be a reminder of the way you used to operate before complexity got the better of you. Or maybe, for the first time in your life, you'll see that the pursuit of excellence can start right now with one small decision, followed by another decision and another and another. It will finally dawn on you that you don't need more hours in the day. You don't need to wait for more opportunities to fall into your lap. Whether you're picking up a pursuit that got sidetracked or starting your pursuit for the first time right now, one decision is all it takes to set the wheels in motion.

CHAPTER ONE

STRATEGIC BEHAVIOR THEORY

"We make progress by eliminating things."

-*Steven P. Jobs*

A few years ago, a crack team of young leaders at a Fortune 100 health insurer joined together for a common purpose. This talented bunch wanted to merge their professional ambitions with their passion for social good. Thus was born The Roundtable. Ostensibly, the Roundtable's goal was to do well by doing good. In practice, that meant improving the quality of healthcare by generating practical, customer-centric solutions that also strengthened their behemoth employer. Within a month, the creative thinkers had deployed their abundant imaginations and information-gathering skills to generate more than 37 great ideas for improving customer health and company profits. During the second month, the team was still hashing over even more new ideas supported by more newly discovered research. The third month brought more information curation. The team's earnest desire to change the world had morphed into a serious case of analysis paralysis.

Does this sound familiar to you? It can be an incredibly frustrating never-ending cycle that gums up the gears of strategy and innovation. Not only have I witnessed scenes like this all across the Corporate World at every level of an organization from the front lines to the executive suites, but I've also participated in them. The speed of change coupled with the pressure to innovate and the increasing use of hastily assembled, temporary project teams leaves people desperately grasping for a simple framework for making complex decisions quickly and strategically.

If you were part of The Roundtable, how would you go about making this decision? What thought process would you use? Would you take the famous Ben Franklin approach and make a simple list of pros and cons for each of the 37 options, canceling out each con with each pro, and see which list ends up longer? (Hope you have a lot of time.) Of course, even if you have time, you will probably realize that some of the pros should count more than the others, and likewise with the cons. Is potential social good worth more or less than a negative financial impact to the company?

So perhaps your inner bean-counter will take over and drive you to a spreadsheet, complete with elegant formulas that assign weighted values to each variable. After much deliberation to decide which variables matter, and even more arguing over how important each variable is relative to the others, you get it figured out. You might list the factors for consideration something like this: Potential for profitability—20%; contribution to social good—20%; value for internal stakeholders—40%; personal satisfaction for our team—10%; ease of execution—10%. That would be your top row. Then you could list each of the 37 possible ideas down the left column, and go to work assigning a score to each idea for each variable. It might take a little while, but eventually you'll get there and you can let the spreadsheet do its magic. Imagine the possibilities!

Heck, maybe this *is* the product. You could package and market the spreadsheet as a nifty tool called the "Decide-O-Matic!"

But then another thought occurs to you. How much can you really trust those numbers? How do you know you captured all of the relevant variables? Could there be another critical factor you completely overlooked? How do you know you assigned the correct weights to each of the variables, let alone assigned the right score to each idea for each of the weighted variables? The spreadsheet may give you a comfortably quantitative result, but what if it is cloaking the true ambiguity under a blanket of false confidence? You're wise enough to know that in reality the method of arriving at those deliciously concrete numbers was riddled with guesses, opinions, compromises, and shaky assumptions. So maybe you could revert to your B-school training and conduct a thorough analysis on the projected costs and revenues for each idea. Yes, that's what a prudent decision maker would do, isn't it? Then you could analyze the competitive landscape and do the same analysis for all of the possible competitors...for all 30 ideas. On second thought, how long will it take to gather all that data? Will there even be a market for the idea by the time you are ready to implement it? And where do we even begin assigning projected financials, dates, and probabilities of success on an innovative idea that by its very definition has never been done before? Not to mention, while this might give you an objectively rational answer, it will say nothing about the unique strategic direction of your company, let alone the strategic direction of your team.

So what is the alternative? If the conventional solutions don't work, then what are you supposed to do? Should you just go with your gut? If so, exactly which team member's gut should you go with since your team has 11 potentially different guts to consider? Maybe you should just accept your helplessness in the face of a random and uncontrollable world and draw an idea out of a hat or flip some coins? For added entertainment value, you could also have the proprietors of each idea arm-wrestle.

In the face of all these different yet equally unsatisfying approaches to deciding, it's easy to see how decision paralysis thwarts progress, derails strategies, and prevents good teams and leaders from making the leap to greatness.

The good news is that there is a better way.

1. Know-Think-Do

I don't know if I can pinpoint when my fascination with decisions first started. But I think it began sometime during my junior high or high school years when I noticed that some kids who had always seemed so similar in their likes, dislikes, interests, and general patterns of behavior began splintering off and choosing wildly different pursuits for themselves, while other kids seemed to let everything be chosen for them by their parents, teachers, or friends. Then I watched *The Breakfast Club*, which obviously explained everything. Nevertheless, by that time I was hooked. When I finally arrived at college, I couldn't imagine studying anything other than psychology. At some point during the first part of my career as a management consultant at Andersen Consulting, what had begun as a personal fascination with decision-making morphed into what my wife (not to mention, many psychiatrists) might label a professional obsession. While working on the mergers of Exxon and Mobil, as well as British Petroleum and Amoco, I saw first-hand that the challenges of decision making which seemed so ubiquitous during my school years were just as prevalent in the real world populated by relatively smart adults. Years later, while the head of research and development at the learning and assessment company, TalentSmart, I was finally able to test my assumptions. After digging through performance data from hundreds of thousands of individuals and teams from all types of industries and organizations spanning the globe, we discovered that indecision was everywhere. Not years of experience, nor Ivy league MBAs, nor high IQ's provided any kind of immunity from chronically indecisive behavior patterns. Shortly after I shared the findings of our research with our client base, GE Capital asked me to spend a few days discussing decision-making with their high potential leaders from around the world. In researching for those early talks, I found that virtually all available decision frameworks either buried the poor decision-maker in unnecessarily complex, time-consuming, and often futile calculations that conveniently ignored the fact that decisions must be made by real people with real jobs in a constantly changing real world environment, or those frameworks paid no attention to the fact that the quality of a decision can only be judged within the context of the decision-maker's strategic objectives. That's when the first seed was planted for the Know-Think-Do framework.

But it remained just that—a seed—for quite a while. Only after continuing to feed my obsession with more research and more application in my organizational consulting and executive coaching work did everything coalesce into a coherent framework that not only explained why people made the choices they did, but also became a tool my clients could actually use to be more effective decision-makers.

Strategic Behavior Theory describes the prescriptive framework I developed for helping my clients think more strategically and act more decisively every day. Like all theories, Strategic Behavior Theory (SBT) is based on a combination of empirical research, as well as observations from my work either studying or facilitating the decision habits and processes for thousands of teams in hundreds of organizations ranging in size from one person small businesses to the world's largest multi-national corporations. In all cases, strategic behavior results from doing three things consistently every single day: knowing, thinking, and doing. Good decisions must begin by *knowing* your strategic direction before *thinking* logically about which options best align with that strategic direction; and finally *doing* something active and decisive with all of those strategic thoughts. As we'll see later in this chapter, all three parts of the framework are equally important for successful decision making, and all three parts also require a willingness to quit. The framework is robust enough to help top executives frame the strategies of Fortune 500 corporations, yet simple enough to guide the choices of everyone from high-potential leaders and consultative salespeople to small business owners and working parents. Although SBT is a "theory" the framework is an eminently *practical* approach to building and sustaining strategic momentum in every area of life and work.

The three critical behaviors in the SBT framework map to a simple three-step process for making decisions strategically. Different people prefer different approaches to each step in the process. Together, your preferences make up your Decision Style. In chapter eight, we'll delve deeper into the individual components.

Behavior	Step in the Process		
1 KNOW	Check your Pulse.	1 — — — — — — — — — 7 Operational — Conceptual	
2 THINK	Consult an Anti-You.	1 — — — — — — — — 7 Risky — Cautious	
3 DO	Be a Decider.	1 — — — — — — — 7 Deliberative — Impulsive	

2. Decisive to the Core

A few years ago, the psychologists Timothy Judge and Charlice Hurst conducted a fascinating study. Partnering with the National Longitudinal Study of Youth, they examined the progress of more than 12,000 people for more than two decades. They were interested in all sorts of advantages and disadvantages that might affect whether a person winds up digging ditches or founding the next Apple Computer. Judge and Hurst looked at obvious things like the occupation of the teenagers' parents. Did they grow up in a blue collar home or a white collar home? Were the teens' parents doctors, lawyers, or dropouts? Did they come from money or poverty? The researchers were also interested in measurables, like which grades the teens earned in high school, and what kind of scores they received on their SATs. When the teens reached their late thirties and early forties, Judge and Hurst took all of that information about their upbringing and academic performance and compared it to their annual income. In general, the results turned out how you might expect. The kids born of wealthy, well-educated parents who graduated near the top of their high school class tended to make more money as adults than the blue collar kids who figured out early on that school wasn't really their bag.

But Judge and Hurst also looked at something else. This is where things get interesting. A unique subset of people in the study did not follow the general pattern. By the time they reached their middle years, some sons and daughters of roofers and plumbers whose grades (ahem) made the top half of the class possible, still ended up making 30-60 percent more money each year than many of their more privileged peers. What this select breed of underdogs had in common was nothing but a unique set of personal beliefs about their ability to shape the future. These beliefs (which relate to emotional stability, internal locus of control, self-efficacy, and self-esteem) translate directly into the ability to choose one course of action while *quitting* others. The higher people scored on these four traits, the more positively they believed they could cope with uncertain and downright unpleasant circumstances. It was that core self-evaluation (CSE) that empowered the group of seemingly disadvantaged teens to rise above both their circumstances and their peers.

A couple of years ago, a psychologist at the University of Michigan named Georges Potworowski performed a study on indecisiveness. One of the things he wanted to find out was whether or not there were any personality traits that made some people more likely to waffle or flat-out refuse to decide at all. What he discovered was that people who score low on many of the same traits measured by the CSE—they are emotionally unstable, they lack confidence and self-esteem—are also more prone to behave indecisively. Potworowski explains his results using a simple example of responding to a party invitation. Imagine your friend Paul is having a party. Paul's more indecisive friends (not you, of course) probably won't RSVP because they are afraid that the second they respond "yes," Peter or Mary will announce an even cooler party on the same day (the horror!). But they don't want to respond "no" either, since Paul's party might turn out to be the cat's meow after all.

Plus, there is a powerful social element. Paul's friends like Paul and want to be liked by him. But they also like Peter and Mary. As a general rule, they like to be liked. They score high on the personality trait of "agreeableness" and low on the trait of "social boldness." In other words, they are really nice, and they don't like to ruffle feathers by rejecting invitations and telling people "no." Nice they may be. But all too often those traits result in a chronic failure to make a decision.

But really, who cares? Failing to RSVP like I am guilty of on occasion might send extra-conscientious people like my wife to an early grave due to unmitigated frustration. In the grand scheme of things it isn't a big deal, is it? The answer is probably "no," if all we are talking about is a cocktail party hosted by unconditionally loving friends. But the inability to make what Harvard ethics professor Joseph Badaracco calls "right vs. right" decisions can be a fatal leadership flaw. An otherwise talented manager who can't bring himself to focus on one customer segment at the expense of others (*but what if they want to buy, too!?!*) winds up taking his team in circles, and his career into a rut.

At the heart of strategic thinking is the ability to focus on one strategy while consciously quitting the pursuit of others. Choosing what we want to do is easy. It's choosing what *else* we want to do that we are nonetheless going to quit doing that is the hard part—to build the school by stripping funding from the hospital; to develop this product while shutting down production of that one. As David Packard (of Hewlett-Packard fame) once said, "more companies die from overeating than starvation." The same truth applies to our careers and personal lives.

In my writing and my speeches, I make a bold claim that decisiveness is *the* single most important success factor for people in today's information-saturated environment. That is exponentially true for leaders who must navigate a team in that environment. Whenever I do this in room full of people, I receive two responses. Most people issue nods of agreement, and others stare back at me with furrowed brows and squinty eyes. The second batch of people view my claim with skepticism. They believe that I'm missing something. To them, what it sounds like I'm saying is that the secret to success is to be more impulsive—to perpetually chase whims and hunches, consequences be damned. If you, dear reader, are one of those skeptics I say to you, "you're right." Even though in *The Impulse Factor* I presented a substantial body of evidence to support the claim that impulsiveness is not the automatic kiss of death that we've all been taught to believe, impulsivity by itself is not an automatic success factor either. Decisiveness and impulsiveness are different. I can sum up that difference in one word: *direction.*

3. The Education of Steve Jobs

"Stop!" Steve Jobs shouted. "This is crazy!"

The scene was a products strategy meeting at the Palo Alto headquarters of Apple Computer in autumn of 1997. More than a decade after his ouster as CEO of Apple in 1985, Steve Jobs was asked by the board of Apple to reclaim his throne as its Chief Executive. When he returned, reviewing the company's product line was a top priority. One by one, Jobs invited every product team to a 90-minute meeting in which they were asked to justify why their product mattered. After sitting in on the flailing computer giant's meetings for three weeks, Jobs grew more and more frustrated with the company's complete and utter lack of direction. Finally, Jobs snapped. As Walter Issacson describes it in his engaging biography, Jobs "grabbed a magic marker and padded to a whiteboard and drew a horizontal line and a vertical line to make a four-squared chart. 'Here's what we need, he continued. Atop the two columns he wrote 'consumer' and 'pro.' He labeled the two rows 'desktop' and 'portable.' Their job was to make four great products, one for each quadrant." Everything else followed a direct path to the recycling bin. Just like that, Steve Jobs eliminated 70% of Apple Computer's product line ranging from printers to personal digital assistants like the Newton. Yes, that's right, the innovative geniuses who would eventually give birth to iPods, iPhones, and iPads began their creative quest by *quitting* the development of handheld devices.

One unfortunate but necessary outcome of that decision was massive layoffs. The company's bloated product line had to be supported by a bloated staff that the company simply could not afford. Following a $1 billion loss the prior year, Apple had been within 90 days of bankruptcy before Jobs slashed the products and the corresponding people. A more pleasant result of the decision was laser focus for the company's top engineers. That focus gave birth to the Power Mac (pro+desktop), the Power Book (pro+portable), the iMac (consumer+desktop), and the iBook (consumer+portable). It also set the stage for perhaps one of the most impressive and successful runs of consumer product creation in recent history. One quarter after the slash and burn session, Apple recorded its first profit in two years. It has since gone on to become the most valuable company in the world with a market capitalization of $620 billion at the time of this writing. At the Apex of Jobs' success, Nike CEO, Mark Parker, asked Jobs if he had any advice for him. Jobs replied "well, just one thing. Nike makes some of the best products in the world. Products that you lust after. But you also make a lot of crap. Just get rid of the crappy stuff and focus on the good stuff." Jobs later told Tiffany Kaiser of dailytech.com that "people think focus means saying yes to the thing you've got to focus on....but that's not what it means at all. It means saying no to the hundred other good ideas that there are. You have to pick carefully."

There is a long list of words that have been used to describe the late Steven P. Jobs. "Humble" and "agreeable" have never made that list. Jobs was unquestionably confident and bold, and he certainly never let the need to be socially agreeable stand in the way of doing whatever he wanted to do. His CSE score would have probably been off the charts…right along with his Narcissistic personality score. His legendary "reality distortion field" is ample evidence that Jobs absolutely believed he could shape the world around him more than the world shaped him. As such, he established a rather infamous history of decisive action. While decisiveness certainly contributed to Jobs' success, it is also what got him booted from his own company in 1985. During Jobs' 12 years in the corporate wilderness, he acquired invaluable judgment and discretion when it came to business strategy and operations. His one-time mentor and Apple Board member, Arthur Rock, claimed that forcing Jobs out in 1985 was the greatest gift the Board could have given him. Jobs' later success was due to his demotion, not in spite of it, Rock believed. Jobs learned how to channel his unique gift for focus and decisiveness not toward personal whims anymore, but on initiatives that made sound strategic sense. In general, letting trees (and bridges) burn was never an activity that emotionally tormented Steve Jobs. But after he returned to Apple's helm, he also revealed a now legendary ability to decide which product ideas should burn, and which should be nurtured. Though he never became known for his tact, Jobs did prove to be highly effective at providing clarity about the strategic direction for his employees. But not because of what he chose to do, because of what he chose to quit.

While flakes and quitters and the generally unreliable are a dime a dozen, people who possess the strength to quit a potentially valuable course of action — even and especially when quitting is emotionally difficult and socially unpopular — are the exceptions and not the rule. But even tough quitters will only win if they develop the skill of knowing *what* to quit. That must be determined by their strategic direction. Any new CEO with a history on Wall Street and a keen eye for cost accounting could have come into Apple in 1997, taken one look at the company's depressing balance sheet and immediately gone on a 1980's style reign of terror—indiscriminately slashing products, divisions, and people. In the short run they too would have returned Apple Computer to profitability. They too would have forced the company to be leaner, and to make every department do more with less. After all, the company needed some pruning. But all of this slashing and burning would have been a short term fix. Absent a clear strategic direction, cost-cutting and reorganization would have been about as useful as trying to trim the costs of a rotary-dial phone to be more price-competitive with a smart phone. It was the combination of Steve Jobs' natural ability to act decisively *and* his clarity of strategic direction that enabled him to effectively decide what to quit so they could truly focus on what to pursue. When he returned to Apple for round two, he brought with him the strategic eye of a master sculptor.

Despite his other shortcomings—and interpersonally, there were many—Jobs did two important things exceptionally well. He defined a clear strategic direction and mandated that everyone act decisively in that direction.

4. The Dynamic Duo

The evidence for Strategic Behavior Theory has emerged over time, thanks to my fortuitous collaboration with people far more gifted than myself. In the case of SBT, there are two people in particular.

As a college undergraduate, I backed into an opportunity to staple papers and enter data for a researcher named Tim Judge, when he was a rising star in academia. While not yet a household name, Judge who is now a professor at the University of Notre Dame's Mendoza School of Business, is one of the most published and respected applied psychologists alive today. Among a long list of fascinating research topics including emotional intelligence and the connection between job satisfaction and job performance, Tim Judge first opened my eyes to the core self-evaluation. That work eventually led to the decisive action piece of Strategic Behavior Theory.

But as we've seen, there is more to SBT than decisive action. A while back, before I wrote my first book, I was working with a group of high potential leaders at GE Capital. We were discussing the merits and downfalls of quick decision making. The group of instinctive decision makers concluded that acting on intuition and the ability to take risks is usually an asset, as long as the action is "directionally correct." In other words, it isn't the size of the risk that matters so much as it is the direction of the risk. Even a small risk that doesn't align with your strategic direction is a problem. But a bigger risk in the direction of your strategy is usually a pretty good idea. For example, under Apple's new four-pronged strategy, a relatively safe product that didn't fit into one of those four critical quadrants was a bad idea. But a product that would cost a lot of money to develop yet fit the criteria for being an "insanely great" product in one of those four categories would be a "directionally correct" risk worth taking. It was risky to let a huge fire burn in Yellowstone, but it was a directionally correct risk given Bill Mott's strategic direction of preserving the forest for future generations, and everything he knew about forest fires and lodgepole pine trees.

The directionally correct argument immediately made sense to me. But it wasn't until a few years later that I found the data to support it. The other fortuitous connection behind SBT was with a man named Kevin Wilde. In early 2011, Wilde, the Chief Learning Officer at the multi-national food maker General Mills was informed of a trend within his company's leaders. One of the company's top executives believed that many of his managers appeared to be missing out on too many opportunities. "Things are going great," the executive assured Wilde. "But I think we're leaving value on the table." His belief was that the economic recession had made leaders more timid than usual, and that this timidity could be preventing General Mills from reaching its true potential.

In the game of leadership development, Kevin Wilde is no ordinary player. Under his guidance, General Mills has become no ordinary company. In 2012, General Mills was named the top company in the world for leadership development by *Leadership Excellence* magazine; the #2 company for leadership by *Fortune Magazine*; #1 in the world for corporate learning by *Chief Learning Officer Magazine*; and Wilde himself was named Chief Learning Officer of the year in 2007. (Full disclosure: Kevin is also on my company, Decision Pulse's board of advisors, which I'm quite sure is the accomplishment he is most proud of.) The point is that leaders at General Mills are not bottom-dwellers who are trying to claw their way out of the basement. Wilde and his organization have a well-deserved reputation for consistently being at the forefront of organizational leadership and talent management practices. They maintain this proficiency in leadership development by never getting too comfortable with where they are. So when some of their executives began to feel a nagging sense that a lack of bold leadership could soon haunt them, they immediately consulted Wilde.

Wilde took their concern seriously. However, he did not amass his impressive list of accolades by operating on hunches and chasing the latest management fads. He did what he always does first. He looked to the evidence. The question he wanted to answer was whether or not this was an isolated observation. Was it "real" in this executive's department but nowhere else? On the other hand, this executive could be serving as the canary in the coal mine providing early warning to a much more important trend throughout the entire organization. Wilde began poring over performance data on more than 20,000 managers at General Mills and beyond. That preliminary search led him to a hypothesis that there were two specific skill sets that get to the core of the "bold leadership" issue. The first skill set he labeled "judgment." Judgment included behaviors such as defining a clear strategic direction for your team, and consistently making smart decisions that supported that direction. The other skill set he called "boldness" was about acting with speed and urgency, and decisively pursuing important projects.

No big surprises so far. You don't need a PhD in organizational behavior to conclude that bold leaders who can focus do better than their lumbering, weak-willed and scatter-brained counterparts. Then again, the so-called "A Players" do a lot of things better than average. The question that matters is whether these skills differentiate average managers from great leaders.

After looking at the overall performance scores for a group of 20,000 managers from around the world at General Mills and beyond, he discovered that boldness by itself was not much of a success trait. Only 1 in 10 managers who scored high on boldness but not on judgment, made the list of the excellent leaders (those leaders at the 90th percentile or above in overall effectiveness as a leader as measured by ratings from their peers, their subordinates and their bosses.) Just as we saw in pre-1985 Steve Jobs, boldness without judgment simply is not enough to create a great leader. If the ability to make decisive moves was all a manager was hanging his hat on, he had only an 11% chance of finding himself in the top echelon of excellent leaders. The situation looked even bleaker for managers who scored high on judgment, but low on boldness. For this thoughtful, but timid bunch, only one out of one hundred found themselves in the elite group of top-performing leaders. At this point, the concern about boldness appeared to be a somewhat isolated issue. Perhaps there was something special about this executive's department that either made his team exceptionally timid, or that made boldness exceptionally critical for their particular function while it wasn't so important in most others? For the company as a whole, it seemed liked a false alarm.

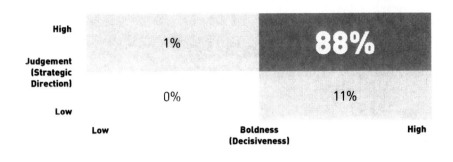

But Wilde didn't stop there. He also wanted to know whether there was any kind of synergistic effect between boldness and direction. Even though these skills alone only gave managers an 11% chance and a 1% chance respectively of becoming an exceptional leader, maybe if a leader had both traits, she could increase her chances to as high as 20% or maybe even 25%? When he analyzed the combination of judgment and boldness together, the results stunned him. For leaders who demonstrated both skills, their chance of being in the top echelon was not just 12% or even 25%. Among those managers who scored high on both direction and boldness, 88% found themselves in the group of exceptional leaders. In practice, this means that if a manager lacks the ability to clearly define and communicate a strategic direction, but is bold, she will every now and then stumble onto something through sheer tenacity and the courage to take risks. But over the long haul, chances are she will be too unpredictable and scattered to become a great leader. On the other hand, while exercising good judgment is certainly better than demonstrating poor judgment, if a leader fails to translate that judgment into decisive action, his chances of becoming a great leader range somewhere between slim and none.

But if you add these two qualities together, you get more than an incremental difference. When combined these two skills increase the odds of extraordinary leadership by a factor of eight.

5. Michael Porter and the Psychology of Blue Oceans

In recent years the concept of "strategic thinking" has taken a starring role in the world of leadership and leadership development. In 2009, an article in the *Wall Street Journal* proclaimed strategic thinking to be the single most important skill of a modern leader. But strategic thinking is a slippery term. Just what exactly does it mean? More to our point here, what does it have to do with quitting?

In regard to his four quadrant product strategy at Apple, Steve Jobs explained that "deciding what *not* to do is as important as deciding what *to* do. That's true for companies and it's true for products." In 2010, Jobs would tell a group of Stanford students that the secret to innovation today was much less about generating new ideas than it was about thinning the herd of existing ideas. "Innovation," Jobs said, "was about saying 'no' to a thousand things." Jobs' view on the necessity of quitting many worthwhile activities in order to fully leverage the potential of a few potentially game-changing ideas echoes the long time stance of Michael Porter, perhaps *the* seminal figure in modern research on business strategy.

Today, Michael Porter is the head of Harvard's Institute for Strategy and Competitiveness. Ever since the early 1980's, Porter's dense body of work has boiled down to one central point: "the essence of strategy is choosing what *not* to do." Yet, it is also the thing that most strategists get wrong. Porter writes that the failure to make these tough decisions comes largely from the pressure to grow or what he calls the growth trap. "Most companies owe their initial success to a unique strategic position involving clear tradeoffs.... the passage of time and the pressures of growth, however, led to compromises that were at first almost imperceptible. Through a succession of incremental changes that each seemed sensible at the time, many established companies have compromised their way to me-too activities just like their rivals...Through incremental additions of product varieties; incremental efforts to service new customer groups; and emulation of rival's activities; the existing company loses its clear competitive position."

Michael Porter is not without his critics. Perhaps the most popular modern alternative to Porter is W. Chan Kim's and Renee Mauborgne's theory of "Blue Ocean Strategy." Professors at France's INSEAD business school, Kim and Mauborgne argue that Porter-like approaches to strategy are too obsessed with competition. They lead organizations to fight their competitors to the death in bloody red oceans, when all the while, tranquil blue oceans of "uncontested market space" are just waiting for smart leaders to find them. Kim and Mauborgne point out many meaningful points of difference between their views and Porter's views with regard to industry structure and competitive analysis. However, in spite of other differences, the Blue Ocean success stories have one important thing in common with Porter's views—tradeoffs. Of course Kim and Mauborgne *claim* just the opposite. They argue that tradeoffs are not essential for creative strategists who can free their mind from the prison of Porter's artificial framework. But when you probe virtually every one of the Blue Ocean examples, you find a strategic leader whose success came largely from choosing what *not* to do.

Take the women's fitness club Curves, for example. Kim and Mauborgne explained that Curves created a blue ocean by "building on the decisive advantages of two strategic groups in the U.S. fitness industry, traditional health clubs and home exercise programs, and eliminated or reduced everything else." Curves said "sorry guys, our clubs are for women only." They did away with fancy locker rooms, spas, saunas, and other pampering frills offered by traditional fitness clubs. Defying conventional industry wisdom, they made enormous tradeoffs by excluding half the potential customer base (i.e. men) for a fitness facility as well as all the other accoutrements of traditional health clubs. Kim and Mauborgne are right that tapping into the advantages of two strategic groups does indeed run counter to Porter's views. In Porter's view, this might be called "straddling," as in trying to keep one foot in two different strategic positions. For Porter this is a no-no. But the last part of the Curves recipe for success— "eliminating or reducing everything else"—is very much aligned with Porter's views about choosing what not to do. Only by making this decision were the owners of Curves able to make its memberships significantly less expensive than other clubs. Only by quitting the practice of co-ed gyms were they able to zero in on the needs of a specific population of women.

Much like reruns of VH1's Behind the Music television show, you will find a recurring pattern in the Blue Ocean stories. Every single example of a blue ocean matches the last part of the Curves story in which they "eliminated or reduced everything else." While there are multiple paths to creating a blue ocean (six, to be specific), every one of those paths eventually intersects with the need to quit doing something significant and traditionally expected before you can reach the shores of a blue ocean. The wildly successful Canadian-born circus/theater act, Cirque du Soleil, quit relying on animals as part of the circus show and did away with staple circus practices such as hiring "stars" like the strong man and the bearded lady. Quitting those costly practices and letting go of the customers who loved the circus for that very reason enabled the company to deliver more artsy entertainment at a lower cost than a traditional circus. Southwest Airlines (an example also used by Porter to support his views) quit offering standard airline industry frills like assigned seating, first class sections, travel agent booking, and in-flight meals in order to create a blue ocean by providing a cheaper air travel option. Porter points out that when Continental Airlines tried to copy Southwest in the early 1990's with Continental Lite, it was a disaster. Why? Because Continental failed to quit doing all of the stuff that forced full service airlines to charge higher fares than Southwest. It was the worst of both worlds—they cut their prices but failed to quit doing the things that kept their costs high. Blue Ocean Strategists might say Continental Lite failed to "reduce or eliminate everything else," which was the key to Southwest's success. So, while Kim and Mauborgne implicitly reject some of Porter's views on industry analysis, choosing to do one thing while "eliminating or reducing everything else" is the textbook definition of the tradeoffs that are the essence of Porter's view on strategy.

My point is simply this: No matter which school of strategic thought you come from, quitting is the one thing you simply must get right if you want to be a great strategic thinker and strategic leader.

Of course, business strategy includes many important nuances that I won't be covering here. Even though I believe we generally overcomplicate what should be a relatively straightforward process, I will concede that there is much more to business strategy than you'll find between the covers of this book. In *Why Quitters Win,* I am purposely adhering to Einstein's dictum that we should "make things as simple as possible, but not simpler." So the question we are trying to answer is, what is the simplest way to ensure sound strategic behavior?

The numbers in Kevin Wilde's research are a good starting point. In terms of real world business impact, you will glean about 88% of the value of strategic thinking by mastering the skills addressed in this book. The ability to forecast future economic trends; conduct a deep industry analysis; create an elegant 63-tab spreadsheet filled with cost and revenue projections; and all the other things we assume are important to strategy will only have about a 12% impact on your ability to generate strategic results if you lack the ability to clearly define a direction and take decisive action. When you get those two things right, then by all means you should learn more about forecasting and industry analysis. But if you want to instantly and noticeably improve your ability to generate strategic outcomes, direction and decisiveness should be your areas of focus. The balance of this book is designed to help you and your team do exactly that by applying the three-part SBT framework.

EXECUTIVE SUMMARY

- Strategic behavior is a person's habitual pattern of thinking strategically and acting decisively every day.

- Strategic behavior results from three simple behaviors repeated over and over again every day with every decision:

1. **Know:** Being clear about your primary strategic direction.

2. **Think:** Logically considering which options align with that strategic direction.

3. **Do:** Taking decisive action.

- Strategic *thinking* is useless without strategic *action*.

- A 25-year study of 12,000 people found that less educated children of blue collar parents who grew up with a decisive mindset made an average of 30-60% higher incomes as middle-aged adults than privileged, well-educated children with an indecisive mindset.

- Another study of 20,000 professional managers revealed that excellent leadership requires both the ability to think strategically and to take bold, decisive action. Only one of out 10 managers who excelled in one skill but not the other turn out to be top-performing leaders, but 88% of managers who excel at both skills are excellent leaders.

- Steve Jobs exemplified both skills with his four-quadrant product strategy that returned Apple to prominence.

- "Deciding what *not* to do is as important as deciding what *to* do. That's true for companies and it's true for products." –Steve Jobs

- Regardless of which perspective you take on strategy, all strategic behavior requires the leaders' to consciously and consistently quit.

CHAPTER TWO

THE ONE-ITEM WISH LIST

"More companies die from overeating than starvation."

--David Packard

Since you are reading this right now, I am going to take a shot in the dark and assume that you currently possess a beating heart. Your heartbeat is the most important thing happening in your body right now. Of course, that is not the only thing happening. Your body performs many important functions. Your muscles enable you to walk, to hug your significant other, and to carry a child. Your mouth allows you to chew food, and to talk to friends and colleagues. Your ears allow you to hear what other people say, to listen to the music on your computer or mp3 player, and to hear cars honking and buzzers beeping. Your brain enables you to ponder life's big questions and to ruminate over all sorts of first-world problems like the low battery life on your Sonicare toothbrush or the way the leather seats in your new Audi get too hot on sunny days. Walking, talking, seeing, hearing and thinking are all very important and magical functions of the human body. But if blood is not pumping through your body, nothing else matters. When your pulse goes, so do you. I don't mean that in some philosophical-higher-plane-of-consciousness kind of way. I mean that in the *your-body-is-now-a-fleshy-paper-weight* kind of way.

Every organization, every team, and every career also has a pulse that reflects the entity's primary strategic direction. Just like the pumping of blood to the muscles in your arms and legs allows you to lift and carry things, the pulse of an organization is what enables it do all of the other things that make it successful. Because of its primacy, the pulse enables leaders to make tough quitting decisions where the right answer is not obvious.

1. How Starbucks Found its Pulse

One cold winter day near the end of January 2008, the founder and newly reinstated CEO of Starbucks Coffee Company, Howard Schultz, made a curious decision. It was a decision that baffled company insiders as much as it did Wall Street analysts.

Starbucks had recently reported a paltry one percent growth from the prior year—its weakest performance to date. In the meantime, the global economy had begun to slow. Despite both of these factors, one of Schultz's first official acts as CEO was to quit on one of the company's hottest products—breakfast sandwiches. With that one decision to remove the sandwiches from Starbucks stores, Schultz irritated millions of loyal customers and killed a product line that accounted for 3% of their annual revenue. Weeks later, he would knowingly cost the company six million more dollars in lost sales by closing down every North American store for an entire afternoon, not to save on labor costs but to conduct a mandatory paid training on how to pour a proper espresso shot. Those two controversial decisions were just the first of many bold decisions that would cause Wall Street to wonder if someone had spiked Schultz's coffee with crazy pills.

But there was a method behind Schultz's madness. He had decided that Starbucks primary strategic direction was reclaiming their position as "the coffee authority." Breakfast sandwiches were threatening that authority.

The story began a few months before, when Schultz walked into one of his beloved Starbucks stores in his home city of Seattle. For a long time, the fair prince of Starbucks believed he smelled something rotten in the state of Washington. Namely, *breakfast sandwiches*. The moment he entered the store that day, he caught the scent of burnt cheddar from a breakfast sandwich in the air. His blood pressure instantly spiked.

The immensely popular breakfast sandwiches had been introduced in 2003 and had sold very well ever since. The problem for Schultz was that every sandwich needed to be heated in a toaster oven. After a couple of minutes, a barista would pull a hot, delicious sandwich out of the oven and hand it to a satisfied customer. Some of the yummy melted cheese would inevitably drip onto the toaster oven grates where it would be charred over and over again for hours every time a new sandwich was heated, releasing a cheesy smell throughout the store. "I immediately felt frustrated because, once again, burnt cheese had enveloped the store," Schultz recounts in his tell-all book, *Onward*. "I spoke to the manager about it. But she did not understand my concerns because she said 'the store had already far exceeded the sales goals for sandwiches that week.' I left the store depressed. What would be next? Hashbrowns?"

Schultz pressed the issue with the company's executive team. Shortly after that fateful day in the Seattle store, he even went so far as to order Michelle Gass, then the head of global products, to "get the sandwiches out." At this time, however, Schultz was not the Chief Executive. That spot belonged to Jim Donald, the man whom Schultz had turned the company's reigns over to a couple of years before. And Jim Donald disagreed with Schultz about the sandwiches. Less than an hour after Schultz issued his demand to Gass, Donald vetoed it. Donald's argument was clear and logical: Starbucks needed the sandwiches. He backed up his view with data, *lots of data*. Market research revealed that Starbucks' customers loved the sandwiches. They provided the company with respectable profit margins and they accounted for over $300 million in sales each year. In recent years, the company had also felt the loss of their less discerning coffee customers who opted for the lower cost—even if lower quality—coffee of McDonald's new McCafe line. Removing the sandwiches would force many of their otherwise loyal customers to go elsewhere for breakfast, even though they really wanted Starbucks coffee. The sum of all this data told Jim Donald that removing breakfast sandwiches would be a big mistake. Financially, it would be like lopping off a big toe in the middle of a marathon. Money aside, eliminating sandwiches would almost certainly drive even more of Starbucks customers into the welcoming arms of Ronald McDonald.

But for Howard Schultz, allowing the smell of cheese to overpower the smell of coffee was near blasphemy. Starbucks was a coffee company in name, in spirit, and also in strategy. It was not a food company. It was not a bakery. It was not a cafeteria.

Somewhere along the way, Schultz believed that the company fell into an identity crisis. As a result, Starbucks had eroded its "coffee authority." Schultz and his team had built an empire by replicating the magic and romance he found so appealing in the Italian espresso bars he first visited back in the 1980's. Within Starbucks, he had built a culture that obsessed about coffee beans and roasting techniques. The company had gone to extraordinary lengths to educate every single in-store barista on the proper way to steam milk and pour an espresso shot. Once upon a time, Starbucks even obsessed about aromas. During their prime, every person who walked into a Starbucks store was greeted by the scent of fresh coffee, rather than assaulted by the odor of burnt cheese. One whiff at a time, Schultz believed they had diluted their coffee authority. "Whatever rich, hearty, coffee aroma that remained was overwhelmed by singed Monterey jack, mozzarella, and most offensively, *cheddar*. I couldn't stand it," Schultz lamented. "Where was the romance in burnt cheese?"

A few months later, with the support of his board of directors, Schultz replaced Jim Donald as CEO and made his first controversial decisions. As predicted, Schultz's decisions initially made Starbucks' financial situation even more precarious. But within eighteen months after reclaiming the throne, despite the persistence of the Great Recession, Starbucks was once again on a growth trajectory that would eventually lead to its highest stock price ever in the summer of 2012. Just like Bill Mott quit trying to protect some of Yellowstone's healthier trees from fires in order to preserve the long term health of the forest, Howard Schultz quit on a profitable product in order to preserve Starbucks' long term sustainability. What enabled him to make that call was his clear understanding of his company's Decision Pulse.

How did Schultz know that Starbucks' Decision Pulse was being recognized as "the coffee authority" and not something else? After all, Howard Schultz firmly believed in the company's mission to "elevate the human spirit." He believed that local Starbucks stores had truly become "the third place" for millions of loyal customers all around the world, behind only their home and their office. Why wouldn't one of those be the Decision Pulse? Even Howard Schultz himself sounds a little fuzzy when he tries to explain it. Schultz writes that in comparison to professional managers, "the founder's perspective is unique. We know what inspired the company and what it took to create it. The knowledge that history brings comes with an intuition about what is right and what is wrong. But sometimes entrepreneurs can be blinded by emotion…whether I was right or wrong about the sandwiches was less telling than my obsession with removing them, which was a manifestation of my mounting frustration. Twenty years after purchasing Starbucks, I felt like a captain who could sense his ship slowly sinking." Later, Schultz explicitly writes that Starbucks is "a people company that served coffee, not a coffee company that served people." In statements like these, it seems that even he doesn't recognize the value of Starbucks' "coffee authority."

It might have been intuition and raw emotion that guided Schultz's decision to remove the breakfast sandwiches and focus on coffee. But I think that years of experience running the business had educated and sharpened his intuition on the fundamentals of strategy. When viewed through a strategic lens, there was something special about being the coffee authority that could not be captured by "elevating the human spirit" or "being the third place."

2. The Value Variance Matrix

At some level, all strategies can be understood as the group's relationship to their competitors and their customers. A Decision Pulse is a concise, actionable statement of that relationship. It successfully answers the fundamental question: *What can we do better than our competitors that our customers highly value?* Answering this question is not just vital for organizations. It is as critical for individual careers as it is for project teams, business units and the heads of multi-national corporations.

The simplest way to capture this relationship is with the Value-Variance Matrix. The vertical axis of the matrix represents the amount of value a given activity or feature provides to your customer. Your customer places some amount of value on everything you do. It might be of low value, high value, or somewhere in between. The horizontal axis represents how much variance there is between your activities and those of your competitors. Every activity you perform or feature you provide is either very similar to your competitors, very different than them, or somewhere in between.

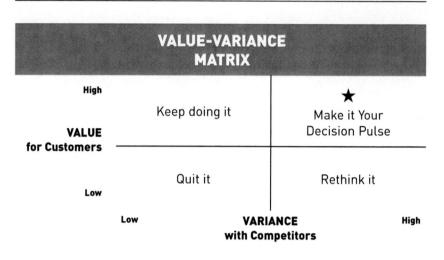

For example, "elevating the human spirit" would probably score high on "value for customers." One homicide detective with the Los Angeles Police Department told Schultz said that he comes to Starbucks for that reason. When the recession hit his household and money became tight, he and his wife discussed whether or not he could give up his daily trips to Starbucks for his coffee. The officer said that his trips to Starbucks had become essential re-energizing escapes from the ugliness inherent in his daily job. His trips to Starbucks were about more than just coffee. He came there to get his spirit elevated.

However, elevating the human spirit scores low on Variance with competitors. It does not differentiate Starbucks from say, Panera Bread, Caribou Coffee or most other coffee chains. So we would place "elevating the human spirit" in the upper left quadrant. To be sure, this value is important to the Starbucks experience and it plays a vital role in connecting the organization to that irresistible human drive for meaning. It is certainly more inspirational than "the coffee authority." That is why a Decision Pulse should exist in addition to a mission statement, and not as a substitute for it. But elevating the human spirit does not make Starbucks uniquely valuable in the way "the coffee authority" does. While there are plenty of other coffee shops who offer premium coffee, there are none that even come close to the scale or notoriety of Starbucks. There are none who devote as many resources (people hours, dollars, or collective energy) to research and development specifically on coffee innovations. It is no accident that Starbucks came up with the world's first non-gag-inducing instant coffee with their VIA brand or that they pioneered Frappuccino. Starbucks can make a legitimate claim to being "THE coffee authority." Even though he may not have explicitly articulated it in value-variance terms, I believe Schultz's intuition had zeroed in on where Starbucks' many different value propositions fit in that schema. If they lost their coffee authority, they would still have nice baristas and a comfortable yet vibrant atmosphere, but they wouldn't be different than scores of other restaurants and jazz clubs who also provide nice employees, snacks, and a comfortable atmosphere that elevates the human spirit.

In the end, the point of the Decision Pulse is not to revolutionize the business of strategy. I'm not trying to convert you to a new school of strategic thought proctored by yours truly. A Decision Pulse should simply make the strategy you already have more actionable for the people in your organization from the CEO on down to the swing shift supervisors. My clients often say it "frames our strategy." If you already have a favorite approach to strategy, you can and should feel free to start there in defining your Pulse.

For Michael Porter fans, your Decision Pulse might be similar to your strategic position. For Blue Ocean strategists, the makings of a Decision Pulse will probably be somewhere in the open waters between your "focus" and your "compelling tag line." For disciples of Jim Collins, your Decision Pulse is a conceptual cousin to your Hedgehog Concept. For still others your Pulse might simply be the most core of your core capabilities or competencies, or your "strategic intent." (The next chapter will help you find your Pulse, in case you're getting curious). And if you have no idea what I'm talking about and think Jim Collins is Jackie's ex-husband, and that Blue Ocean strategies refer to marine biology, that's okay. I am a management geek largely so you don't have to be. Just stick with what you've learned here about the Decision Pulse.

No matter where you find your Pulse or what else it is similar to, the only indisputable criteria of your Decision Pulse is that it absolutely positively must be specific and *actionable* for people other than you or your immediate leadership team. People must be able to use it to make strategic decisions. When every person throughout the organization can put their finger on a Decision Pulse and feel it pounding, strategic momentum is almost inevitable. This is precisely what happened at the British fashion icon, Burberry.

3. Back to the Trenches

A couple of years before Howard Schultz made his triumphant return to the company he founded and the brand he personally built, a very different exchange of power was taking place across the

Atlantic. To see Angela Ahrendts today, you would be tempted to conclude she was clearly a perfect fit for the top job at Burberry. A slender woman with sandy blonde hair and defined facial features, Ahrendts looks like she might have once modeled for the company she now leads. In reality, however, Ahrendts seemed to many like an odd choice. Born, raised, and educated in rural Indiana—thousands of miles from any of the world's fashion centers, let alone London— Ahrendts seemed like one of the last people qualified to return a storied British fashion brand back to global prominence.

Unlike Howard Schultz or Steve Jobs, Angela Ahrendts did not start Burberry. She wasn't there when a scrappy 21 year old entrepreneur named Thomas Burberry founded the company that continues bearing his name more than a century later. Ahrendts wasn't there in 1901 when Burberry created a specially designed coat for English military officers, which turned out to be the perfect outerwear for World War I soldiers assigned to represent their country's interests under the miserable conditions of trench warfare. The Burberry "trench coat" as it became known ended up becoming a mainstay in the British wardrobe for the rest of the 20th Century—a staple for movie stars, explorers, and royalty. That is why Angela Ahrendts was so stunned to see what her top leadership team was *not* wearing at her first strategic planning meeting at Burberry. "They had flown in from around the world to classic British weather, gray and damp, but not one of the more than 60 people was wearing a Burberry trench coat." Ahrendts believed this was the primary reason why, in spite of a booming global fashion industry, Burberry was only growing 2% per year. "The company had an excellent foundation, but it had lost its focus in the process of global expansion," Ahrendts wrote.

Armed with these insights, Ahrendts and her team began doing their homework about others in the industry. What they found was that Burberry was virtually the only successful global luxury brand not capitalizing on the product that made it famous. Despite diversifying, most of Louis Vuitton's sales still came from luggage. Gucci still earned most of its money from leather goods. Burberry's flagship outerwear, on the other hand, accounted for only one-fifth of Burberry's global business. Much like breakfast sandwiches at Starbucks, Burberry's trademark checkered accessories had begun distracting its team from its true core. Ahrendts didn't ban the manufacture of checked clothing in the way that Howard Schultz halted all sales of breakfast sandwiches. Ironically however, the woman born in America's heartland made it clear that under her watch Burberry would be obsessively focused on "our heritage, our Britishness." Ahrendts believed that trench coats were the one thing that its customers highly valued that also set them apart from their competitors. Upon that sturdy outerwear foundation, she believed they could build a thriving global brand.

Although most of Ahrendts' team agreed with the new direction, not everyone felt it was the path to the promised land. Both inside and outside the company, many people were skeptical. After all, wasn't the checked pattern the symbol of Burberry? And who even wore trench coats anymore? Ahrendts recalls, "I'm sure they left saying, *focusing on trench coats—that's our strategy?*" Yes, indeed it was their strategy. As a result of that strategic direction, over the past five years Burberry has tripled its headcount, while doubling both its sales and its profit.

So what is the big takeaway of the dramatic stories at Starbucks and Burberry? Is it that returning to your heritage is the key to success in business and in life? There is something to that. But while reflecting on your heritage is usually a helpful exercise, it is not the main point. Neither is the main point that diligently studying your offerings and plotting them on the Value-Variance Matrix is the only way to reveal the one clear and irrefutable value proposition for your company or your career. The Value-Variance Matrix is a helpful tool, but the vital point of this chapter is even simpler. I think the big idea is captured perfectly by a remark from Angela Ahrendts in which she says, "the decision to focus on our heritage opened up a wealth of creativity."

Did you catch it? She said, "the decision to focus." The decision to focus is the secret to unlocking the power of any group of people whether a high-tech startup, a stalwart charity, a church, a family, or a multi-national corporation. Focusing on your heritage is a great place to start because many of the raw materials are already in place. But even if you don't have a heritage because you are brand new, or even if your heritage is something your group needs to forget, you can still find a Decision Pulse to focus on. You can still define a single strategic direction.

At the risk of being asked to return my pledge pin to the Secret Society of Strategy Consultants, I'm going to share with you a secret: Picking the *right* strategic direction is often less important than picking *a* strategic direction. As much as I love the mental exercise of strategizing and trying to help others figure out what exactly is the strategic direction that will best position them for success, I've become convinced that the most powerful decision is simply the decision to focus, period. Whether you go left or go right at any one point in time usually has less to do with your eventual success than how well your team adapts once you start down the path—regardless of which path you take. As the now controversial Jack Welch candidly put it in his book *Winning*: "In real life, strategy is actually very straightforward. You pick a general direction and implement like hell." What Welch meant is that you pick something that the whole team can focus on. Then you execute and adapt as you go. What he did not mean is that you should spend countless months obsessing and data-crunching and double-checking your facts and getting second opinions and doing endless market research to come up with the *perfect* direction. If you want to unlock the creativity of your team, and to start seeing your people make better decisions every day, then spend a few weeks testing your assumptions and gathering some basic facts, then pick a general direction that reflects what makes you uniquely valuable to your customers. Then focus. Focus like your livelihood depends on it. Focus on something new. Focus on something old. If it makes you feel better, pay someone to tell you what to focus on. Just focus on *something.* Your team will reward you for it.

4. The One-Item Wish List

Imagine for a second that you are a marketing manager at a major U.S. airline. You have just received the results from a customer feedback report you administered a few weeks ago. According to the report, a substantial number of customers on one particular flight responded that they would like to be served a meal. At the moment, you do not offer a meal on that flight. You are thinking about recommending that the company offer a chicken Caesar salad on the flight.

Your task is simple: Make a decision. Do you recommend the salad or not?

Okay, since you are the marketing manager, you would probably know that this company's mission statement says it is "dedicated to the highest quality of customer service delivered with a sense of warmth, friendliness, individual pride, and company spirit." What can we deduce about this company from the mission statement? Well, obviously customer service is tantamount here. They even spell out what customer service in particular means here. It's about warmth and friendliness. It seems like this is probably one of those companies where they say stuff like "Yes,' is the answer. What's the question?"

Armed with that knowledge, what is your decision? Do you listen to the customer feedback and serve the salad?

If you're like most people, you would say "yes." After all, given the information you have available, and everything you've ever been taught about business and customer service, choosing to serve the salad is about the only logical thing a good businessperson could decide. Unless, of course, you know the company's Decision Pulse.

This is not an entirely fictitious situation. It comes from a very real, very successful airline. The ever-quotable and infinitely colorful former chief of Southwest Airlines, Herb Kelleher, once told political strategist, Paul Begalla, "I can teach you the secret to running this airline in 30 seconds. This is it: Southwest is the low-fare airline. Not *a* low-fare airline. We are *THE* low-fare airline. Once you understand that fact, you can make any decision about this company's future as well as I can.

"Here's an example.... Tracy from marketing comes into your office. She says her surveys indicate that passengers might enjoy a light entrée on the Houston to Las Vegas flight. All we offer is peanuts and she thinks a nice chicken Caesar salad would be popular. What do you say?

"You say 'Tracy, will adding that chicken Caesar salad make us *THE* low-fare airline from Houston to Las Vegas? Because if it doesn't, we're not serving any damn chicken salad.'"

The real power of a Decision Pulse is that it cascades throughout an organization. It provides a kind of direction that empowers managers to make the unobvious choices inherent in strategy execution. If you were Tracy from marketing, how would you know that listening to customers was not the right thing to do? If you were the confused manager at the Seattle Starbucks who was crushing the sales goals on breakfast sandwiches, why would you ever think that that very profitable smell of cheese would be a problem for the CEO unless you know that the Decision Pulse is about coffee first?

A Decision Pulse makes a strategy *actionable* for two reasons. First, it tells everyone from the top leader to the front line supervisor how to decide in our organization between what to keep and what to quit. Out of all the ways Herb Kelleher could have illustrated what he meant by being "THE low-fare airline," he chose an example that revealed what they would *not* do in order to maintain their position. Kelleher anticipated the type of scenario that would most likely make even his smartest people stumble—the situations in which listening to the customer is not actually the right thing to do. It would have been almost impossible for Tracy from marketing not to understand the strategic direction after Kelleher's very counterintuitive response. The insight would have hit Tracy from marketing right between the eyes. As a result of that, Tracy could then go back to the marketing department with a crystal clear understanding of the company's direction and how it applies to real world decisions. Tracy would have been on her way to a career as an excellent leader, well-equipped to clarify and focus.

This isn't just lip service at Southwest Airlines, either. I almost always use this example as a short case study in my speeches and Decision Day group sessions. I ask the audience to assume they are Tracy and then make a decision based on the company's mission statement and values. In all of those presentations, I've had only one person select the right answer prior to me revealing the Decision Pulse. Not coincidentally, she happened to be a business development director at Virgin Airlines who had spent the previous eight years at—you guessed it—Southwest Airlines. The point is that everyone at Southwest knew what made their company hum. Yes, as the "LUV" stock symbol implies, love and friendliness is important at Southwest, and so is having fun and not taking yourself too seriously. But it is their dogged attention to low fares that ultimately keeps Southwest Airlines flying. Without that, everything else falls apart. With it, everything can fall into place. The Decision Pulse has to be specific enough to clarify the unobvious "right versus right" decisions.

The second reason why the Decision Pulse enables action is because it is explicit. It is not a list of things. It is one thing—one organizing principle for an entire organization's thoughts and decisions. Any manager can create a strategic plan. But only the most effective leaders have the courage to clarify one strategic focal point. Many leaders are tempted to include everything but the kitchen sink in the strategy they communicate to their teams.

Reducing your focus to only one thing matters far more than most of us tend to think. To illustrate, let's get personal. Imagine your significant other's birthday was coming up in a few weeks. One night over dinner, you ask what gift you could get to commemorate this very special occasion for your partner. You then discover that he/she would like one of the following items: an iPod, tickets to the event he/she would like to go to with you, a new watch, an iPhone, or a new digital camera. All items are priced within your budget.

Then a few days later, you find yourself meandering through the mall when all of the sudden you come across a great deal on a flat-screen TV that you are sure your significant other would love. The television seems like a double-winner. Not only is it a great item in its own right, it also shows how thoughtful you are because you took the initiative to find something that wasn't even on the list! When your significant other's birthday finally arrives, you are beaming with so much pride that you fail to notice the disappointed eyes above the fake smile. If you are like me, you would be oblivious to the clear disappointment and continue thinking, "Wow, I might actually be the world's greatest husband. Seriously, THE best." Meanwhile, behind pursed lips, my wife is thinking, "I thought I told him what I wanted? Why did he even ask me if he was going to get something else, anyway?"

This is the scenario that Harvard Business School researcher Francesca Gino and her colleagues recently presented to hundreds of people in a series of experiments. What they found is exactly the opposite of what most of us think. When we give someone a gift they didn't explicitly request, we think it shows how thoughtful we are. Because of the extra time and effort it took to find this hidden gem, we convince ourselves that the receiver will appreciate our extra-thoughtful gift more than one that he/she requested. The truth is just the opposite. Recipients of a gift (brace yourself for this revelation) appreciate getting the gifts they asked for more than the "thoughtful" gifts they did not ask for. Shocking, isn't it? As the gift-givers, we have it all mixed up. Since it's the thought that counts, we think more thought should count more...never mind what the other person actually wants. Gino summarizes her results saying that "gift givers often go the extra mile to be more thoughtful (e.g., they choose a gift not included on a pre-established gift registry or wish list), they do not realize that sticking to the list would actually come across as more thoughtful and therefore elicit stronger feelings of appreciation."

In addition to explaining why so many of my family's birthday and holiday celebrations have been spoiled by my inept gift-giving, I think Gino's study also reveals something important about the relationship between leaders and the decisions of his or her teams. When a member of your team uses their creative license to do something they *imagine* will provide value in a way you had not actually requested, it creates a serious disconnect. The team members imagine being showered with accolades and bonuses because they went above and beyond the call of duty. The leader, on the other hand, thinks to herself, "Why didn't they just do what I asked them to do? Weren't they sitting right here with me when we laid out our strategic priorities for the year?"

During a six-month global tour to get acclimated at Burberry, Angela Ahrendts recalls visiting a design director and her team in Hong Kong. Bursting with pride, the director's team unveiled the broad array of new shirts they were designing for next season. All of the shirts had the famous Burberry check pattern. Conspicuously absent from the lineup of polo shirts and long sleeve button-downs was a single trench coat. You can almost see that poor design director and her team preparing for Ahrendt's visit with weeks or months of painstaking obsession about the exact color shades to use in the check patterns and conducting a dizzying amount of market research to decide whether to make the collars on the polo shirts a fraction of a centimeter thinner or wider. All the while, they imagined how much their thoughtfulness and attention to detail would be appreciated and rewarded by their new boss. In truth, all Ahrendts really wanted to see was a coat.

Gino's studies indicate a fundamental asymmetry between what we *think* will please people and actually what *will* please them. Sadly, the gift-giver unnecessarily wastes a bunch of time looking for an especially thoughtful gift that the receiver will ultimately appreciate *less* than a gift that he/she clearly said they wanted. When I hear managers say, "I don't like surprises," I think this is what they mean. They do not mean that they want team members to surprise them with a "gift" that wasn't on their strategic wish list. They want their teams to stick to the focal point.

The problem is that leaders often make the wish list too long and ultimately undermine their own request. In follow-up experiments, Gino's team discovered that the longer your wish list, the less likely you are to receive any gift from the list at all. When your wish list includes an iPod, a smartphone, a digital camera, a new watch, or tickets to the game, you are likely to end up getting a TV or a great stereo. But when your list includes only the digital camera, you are likely to get a digital camera. When you present a long list of requests, it appears to the giver that no single item on your list is particularly important. The gift-giver implicitly assumes that basically you just want some electronic device or another. The same is true when leaders identify 17 strategic initiatives for the year that share no clear unifying direction. None of them seem particularly important or unique so it is easy for team members to feel as if they can mix and match "value-added activities" however they like. Why not sell more breakfast sandwiches? Why not start serving an in-flight meal? Why not create a cool line of shirts and some new pairs of trousers with our company's trademarked plaid?

But when you list only one thing, there is little confusion about what you want. People won't stray from the list. They will get creative. They will search high and low, flexing their innovation muscles to provide you with that one thing.

A 2011 study by McKinsey & Company reported that "even at the healthiest companies, about 25 percent of employees are unclear about their company's direction. That figure rises to nearly 60 percent for companies with poor organizational health." I would be willing to bet that every single one of the companies in that McKinsey study had a strategic plan. So why didn't their managers know the direction? The strategic planners' desire to convey a thorough strategy usually means that they create a strategic wish list that is far too long for the executors of that strategy—the lower level teams throughout the company. By trying to define everything, their "wish list" goes on and on and fails to make clear the most important thing—the Decision Pulse. The most important elements and priorities get lost in translation because they are buried in a pile of other initiatives and priorities. As a result, most teams in an organization busy themselves with all sorts of initiatives that "add value" in some vague, vanilla kind of way—an operational improvement here, a cost cut there, productivity increased over there—but ultimately do very little to advance the overall strategy. Think of the sales manager who leads his team to hunt for price-sensitive customers because that's what he has always done to meet his revenue targets, even though the new strategy is now to make the company the premium service provider. Think of the plant manager who pushes his team for higher productivity when the top priority is to improve employee retention. More customers are good. Higher productivity is good. But generally speaking, "good" is irrelevant in the context of a sound strategy. There are many "good" things an individual can do in any organization, but the only "good" that matters are those actions that align with the same Decision Pulse that everyone else in the company is focusing on. For those organizations that successfully align the decisions made by people at every level of the organization with the overall strategic direction, the impact is powerful and quantifiable. The McKinsey report showed that these organizations are twice as likely to have above average financial performance, which is to say nothing about the increased engagement and fulfillment felt by the people within the organization.

In order to achieve that alignment and the resulting success, leaders have to first quit assigning all initiatives equal billing. During the planning phase and every day thereafter, leaders have to make the tough strategic decisions about what they are *not* going to focus on this year. Trimming the list of top priorities down to only one requires officially and explicitly reducing the importance of previously listed "top" priorities, and quitting on others until further notice.

So far we have focused primarily on the Decision Pulse at the corporate level. What if you aren't a CEO? What if you don't get to be involved in setting the strategy of your entire organization? The same truths we've just covered in this chapter apply every bit as well to leaders and teams anywhere within an organization. Whether you're a department head, a store manager, or the leader of a 3-person team consisting of Me, Myself, and I, you have a Team Decision Pulse. In the next chapter, we'll bring it to the surface.

EXECUTIVE SUMMARY

- A Decision Pulse is the primary strategic direction of a team or an organization. It answers the question: *what do we do that our customers value most, and that is also unique to our competitors?*

- Like a beating heart is the most essential function of your body, a Decision Pulse defines the one thing that is most critical to your organization's or team's existence.

- Your Decision Pulse empowers teams and organizations to decide what to *quit* doing. Howard Schultz defined Starbucks' Decision Pulse as "The Coffee Authority" which allowed him to make the tough decision to quit selling breakfast sandwiches.

- The Value-Variance Matrix helps you determine the strategic difference between a mission statement, which describes something your customers appreciate, and your Decision Pulse, which describes what your customers appreciate and what makes you unique and different.

- Angela Ahrendts returned Burberry to global prominence by giving the organization one thing to focus on—trench coats.

- The One-Item Wish List explains Francesca Gino's research revealing why providing a shorter wish list is more likely to get others to give you what you want.

- Herb Kelleher's chicken salad story clarified Southwest Airline's Decision Pulse of "THE low-fare airline" so that his team members would always know the one supreme guiding principle for any strategic decision.

CHAPTER THREE

DISCOVER YOUR TEAM PULSE

"There is nothing so useless as doing efficiently that which should not be done at all."

--Peter Drucker

Not long ago, Randy Ross was recruited to be the head of Human Resources at G&K Services, one of North America's leading uniform and facilities service providers. CEO Doug Milroy had brought Ross into the company in order to make some significant changes in the way the company managed its human capital processes. Ross had a reputation for forward thinking and a history of innovating the people processes within organizations like Best Buy and Target, as well as in mid-sized companies that had outgrown their antiquated human resources systems. He was perfect for the job.

At the time I started working with Ross, he had already developed a well-organized human capital plan with four areas of strategic focus. They wanted to create a culture of service excellence; to develop their high potential leaders; to improve labor relations; and to increase workplace safety. Each of those four areas of focus had eight or nine specific objectives and activities. The entire plan could fit on a single page. Relative to most strategic plans for a 104-person department responsible for serving 7,800 employees, this was awfully concise.

However, Ross was not fully satisfied with his plan yet. He had been around long enough to know how great strategies can wither once exposed to the harsh light of everyday work and the complexities of human thought. In addition to being an executive, Ross also holds a Ph.D. in psychology and is a licensed therapist. He understands the inner workings of the human mind better than most in the business world. So, he suspected that his plan had not done enough to convey the significance of the changes he wanted to make within the department. After all, developing leaders, engaging employees, and keeping unions at bay is pretty standard HR practice at many organizations. And hadn't this been what many of the team leaders had been doing for more than a decade there? Could anyone in the department really be faulted if they looked at this very concise strategic plan and then went back to performing business as usual? He needed something to clarify the fundamental change in direction. He needed a focal point. He needed a Team Pulse.

A Team Pulse is just like the Decision Pulse for an organization, except that it is specific to a team within the larger organization. The Team Pulse should reflect how the members of this team should connect their daily decisions to the company's overall strategic direction. At Starbucks, the supply chain team probably approached "the coffee authority" pulse from a different angle than the district manager of Starbucks retail operations in Southwest Florida simply because the supply chain had to focus on logistics every day, and the other had to focus on a certain kind of customer every day. All Team Pulses should somehow reflect the Decision Pulse of the organization, but they can and should be slightly adapted to fit the specific functions this team performs. To reiterate, the one and only purpose of a Decision Pulse is to clarify decisions. So the Pulse cannot be too lofty or too far removed from what a person actually does on a daily basis. If your organization's Decision Pulse has something to do with serving customers well, then every team needs to understand clearly how they contribute to that Pulse even when they can go months without every seeing a customer, let alone serving one. That's why it is essential for every team in an organization to define their specific Team Pulse.

The process for identifying your Team Pulse has four steps. The first part of the Team Pulse process works like a compass for helping your team find its direction within the organization's larger strategic plan. In less than a single day, Ross and his core team of 17 senior managers and directors uncovered a crystal clear Decision Pulse for their department. Here's the process I used to help them reach that clarity. As we go through it, think about how you would answer the questions for your team, regardless of whether you run a company, lead a division, manage a team, or you are a team of one.

1. Who is your customer?

The first thing we did was to pose a simple question to the group. Who is your customer? In a marketing discussion, this is a fairly common question to ask, but it is rare outside of marketing. After all, the finance teams, Human Resources team, the teams at the manufacturing plants, and virtually everyone outside of sales and marketing typically have no contact with the customer. However, every team has a customer. For this Human Capital team, many possibilities emerged. It could be the buyers of the company's product. Or maybe it was the company's employees? Could it be each other?

When you pose the question a slightly different way, the answer becomes clearer. Who gets to make the final decision about whether or not you succeeded this year, and what do they care most about? For most teams within a corporation, the appropriate "customer" is often that decision maker or group of decision-makers who determine that team's budget. As the old aphorism states, "He who holds the gold, makes the rules." In other words, who is in charge of allocating the resources your team needs to do the things you want with the great people you want to have on your team? That is your customer. To put it another way, at the end of the year, who will decide how much you contributed to moving the company's strategy forward? Often times the people you are most directly serving do not get a vote in this decision. For Ross's team, it was the CEO who would ultimately decide how valuable the Human Capital department's contribution was to the company. At the end of the year, neither the individual employees of the company nor the end users of the company's products and services will get asked to rate the performance of the human resources department. They will not get to decide whether or not the contribution that department makes is so valuable that they need a bigger budget. At the end of the year, the CEO will make that decision.

2. What Is Your Customer's Ultimate Strategic Objective?

As a team leader you might be thinking that all of this sounds great, except for the fact that you don't know what your organization's Decision Pulse is. Furthermore, you aren't in a position to determine it or even to ask the CEO what it is. So how are you supposed to align your team's Pulse with the organization's? Undoubtedly, it is easier if the executive team has already stated a clear Pulse, but that is sometimes a luxury you don't have. Without exception, however, I have yet to meet a manager at any level of an organization who can't answer this question: what is your CEO's ultimate strategic objective for this year? It might be a couple of things, and they might not have been referred to by the executive team as the top priority. But I have yet to work with a team who was not aware of the one or two key goals that everyone in the organization knows about. Here is where we uncover a Decision Pulse in the company's strategy. For Ross and his team, the question was this: At the end of the year, if we as a company move the needle on one thing and nothing else, what would the CEO wish that one thing to be? After more debate and input from executives outside of the HR department, it became very clear that the company's top strategic objective was to become the premium service provider in their industry.

Essentially, what we had done was to very quickly determine that the organization's Decision Pulse was "THE provider of Service Excellence" in their industry. After an in-depth analysis of the company, its competitors, and their customers, the company's executive team determined that relative to their competitors, they vacillated between third and fourth in total market share, but were at the top of their industry in customer satisfaction ratings. We had uncovered the Decision Pulse that every team in the organization needed to focus on. This, of course, was made easier by Ross's understanding of the strategy and the communication of that priority throughout the organization by the CEO. In most cases, however, it's been my experience that virtually all teams within a typical organization already know what the company's Decision Pulse is at some level. They just need to be asked the right questions to uncover it.

With that knowledge, we were ready to begin determining what the Decision Pulse was for their team in particular.

3. What Do You Do That Adds Value to Your Customer?

Typically, a team simply generates a brainstormed list of all of the activities they do and outcomes they achieve that provide the company with value. However, since Ross and his team had already laid out a concise Human Capital Plan with four areas of focus and a total of 34 specific objectives spread out among the four, we already had the list. From there, each of the team members had an opportunity to select which of those 34 objectives were the most valuable to the company strategy. Of the original 34 objectives, 11 of them received at least one vote. From that list of 11, we then asked each team member to rank the top three most important objectives. (To avoid GroupThink and to secure some measure of objectivity, it's important that team members do their rankings independently before sharing them with the rest of the group.)

After going through this process, the top three objectives became clear to the team. Here is where the discovery process officially ends and the decision phase begins.

4. Decide Which of Those Value Statements Makes You Unique.

Typically, by the time we reach this step in the process, it becomes obvious what the Team Pulse should be. The previous discussions have unearthed something that everyone agrees is the most important consideration for the team and its near future. But just as often, the team successfully whittles its way down to three or four possible candidates for the Team Pulse. Ross's team listed things such as "we attract, hire, and retain leaders who create an environment where employees can deliver the Customer Promise" and "Leaders understand, model, and coach how to live and lead the Core Values." At the top of their list was: "Our HR Team's Service Excellence Brand is recognized and sought after." That statement was the one they chose for their Team Pulse. Note how the Team Pulse for Ross's team aligns with the Decision Pulse of the organization as a whole which was to be "the number one provider of service excellence" in their industry. Ross' Team Pulse wasn't *exactly* the same as the organization's Decision Pulse. That is as it should be. Since nobody in the Human Resources department has any direct contact with customers, delivering service excellence to the company's customers would have been almost useless for guiding this team's decisions. For Ross's team, the Team Pulse connected the dots between the company's general strategic direction and the HR department's day-to-day activities.

At some basic level, your Team Pulse must reflect what your team does that is unique within your organization. Ross' team had to figure out what Human Resources would provide their customer (CEO, Doug Milroy) that nobody else in the organization could provide. Ross and his team quickly realized they had a unique opportunity. "We knew HR at G&K could be so much more than company cops," Ross said. "What if instead of being the people who say 'no' all the time, we could be the talent management experts who positioned the company for years of profitable growth? What if we were the group who drove Service Excellence from the inside out starting with the interactions we facilitate with company employees?" In this case, the Team Pulse probably sounds like it is bleeding over into the vision statement for the department. In some ways, it might be. Nothing says that a Team Pulse cannot also be inspirational. It is just vital to remember that inspiration is not the purpose of a Team Pulse. Focus is the purpose.

This is where a Team Pulse takes a conceptual detour from the Decision Pulse for an organization. For internal teams, the idea of what makes you different than your competition is less important. With the Team Pulse you are simply trying to identify the single overarching goal or highest priority initiative that everyone on the team can contribute to.

Since focus is the primary purpose, most Team Pulses turn out to be something more like "stabilize the IT system." Although much less glamorous than "make our Service Excellence brand sought after," this was a highly effective Team Pulse for the Global Asset Management team within a Canadian bank I work with. After going through the same Team Pulse discovery process Ross's team went through, the bank's GAM team determined that there was nothing else they could work on for the next year that would contribute more to the company's strategic direction than getting their information storage systems stabilized. It might not be sexy, but it was incredibly unifying for their team. While vision is certainly an asset for a leader, strategic clarity is more important. There is something of a myth that modern day leaders must also somehow be poets. But strategic clarity and compelling visions don't require flowery language and lofty aspirations. Randy Ross has a big personality. He can't help but inspire. As one of his direct reports puts it, "When you walk into a room with Randy in it, you feel like you are the one sober person who showed up late to a party where everyone else is drunk." If you've met Ross, you know that insight is a compliment. Ross's natural charisma creates an atmosphere that is unexpectedly jubilant because it is so often in stark contrast from wherever it is you just came from.

We all know people like Randy Ross. We also know that most people are not like that. Attempts at charisma for the non-charismatic leader usually come across as stilted and inauthentic. The good news is that good Team Pulses and good leadership don't always require charisma or even world-changing inspiration. What they do require is clarity. Personally, I am all for changing the world.

About every other day, I get a lump in my throat when I hear about a vision to do just that. But trying to shoe-horn inspiration into a Team Pulse can be counterproductive if it causes you to replace clarity with buzz words and platitudes that don't mean much of anything to your individual team members.

It has been my experience that most organizations and most teams within those organizations already have a Decision Pulse or a Team Pulse. It is simply hidden. The Pulse gets lost in the thicket of other value propositions, core competencies, strategic objectives, mission statements, core values, capabilities, and so on. In that way, you don't really *create* a Decision Pulse. You *uncover* the Decision Pulse that was always there.

5. The Pulse Tree

The Team Pulse process enabled Randy Ross to get his team all rowing in the same direction while working through a challenging realignment of the department. Any kind of reorganization will create tension and distraction among team members, simply because of the inherent uncertainty involved. Due in part to his psychology training, Ross wisely recognized that clear direction can relieve much of the emotional tension, while also providing team members with a simple, shared set of criteria on which to base each of their own team's decisions. The common criteria empowered them to create what Michael Porter would call "strategic fit" with the organization's Decision Pulse of being "THE premium service provider." Prior to this, Ross's talent acquisition team knew that they were supposed to be finding good employees. But *good* in what way? The leadership development programs were supposed to be creating good leaders. But *good* in what way? The compensation and benefits department knew they were supposed to be making sure employees got paid and filled out their benefits enrollment documents. But was that all?

After determining the Team Pulse, every member of the team knew precisely how to carry out Ross's strategy. The leadership development directors now knew that they weren't just trying to create generically "good" leaders who knew the ins and outs of textiles and logistics, but leaders who could very specifically create environments where premium service could flourish. It was their job to ensure that leaders didn't just know how to motivate employees to work hard or be more productive, but to motivate them to deliver premium service to customers. Similarly, the recruiters knew that when all else was equal between two qualified job candidates, they should push for candidates who knew a lot about premium levels of customer service. The unspoken rule for the compensation and benefits people who would lead the company's new human resources service center became "no bad experiences." Their primary objective for benefits enrollment was not just efficiency or accuracy, but to make the process as easy and user-friendly as possible so that employees would then be more likely to pass on that level of service to customers. Technical proficiency was a baseline skill required for them, but the ability to provide great service was now the differentiator for people in that department. To be sure, each of these changes were only slight shifts to what

Ross's talented team was already doing. But the sum total of all these slight shifts all throughout an organization is exactly what a Team Pulse looks like in action. The collection of Team Pulses is what ultimately creates strategic fit within an organization.

In a typical team, everyone has a general understanding of which objectives and activities are important to the team. Each of these objectives represents a different direction in which a team member could move in. In practice what you often get is something that looks like the diagram below. Everyone is working on objectives that are "important" but they aren't working on the same objectives at the same time. So, the team is constantly being pulled in multiple directions, and ultimately making very little progress on the primary strategy.

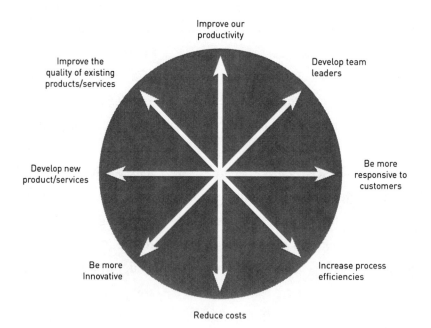

This is the fatal shortcoming of most strategic plans. They end up being treated by managers throughout the organization more like a strategic smorgasbord than a game plan. Imagine the organization as one big cafeteria. The strategic plan is like a big buffet, and the chief executives are the lunch ladies. Each manager goes through the line examining the list of objectives and thinks "Let's see… for my team, I'll take two helpings of product improvement, one helping of leadership development, no cost-cutting or innovation for me this year, thank you, maybe just a dollop of customer focus, and….oh, well, it looks like our plate is pretty full." Then they take their plate back to the table where their team waits to be fed. I think part of the reason the strategic planners take this approach is because choosing one primary objective feels like you're giving up on all of the other objectives that are now lower priority. And to a certain extent, they are right. The strategic planners must consciously quit on some reasonably good strategic objectives to enable the rest of the organization to focus on getting the most important objectives completed. To build momentum for your team in one direction this year, you have to quit moving in multiple directions.

After a team works through the Decision Pulse process, the activities and objectives should look something like this. You can think of the diagram on the next page as a Pulse tree.

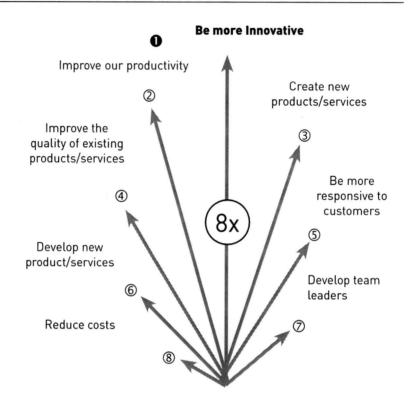

As a rule of thumb, your Decision Pulse (the #1 objective) should guide eight times as many decisions as the #8 objective. In other words, just because you want to be innovative does not mean you should completely ignore cost considerations. But it does mean that the vast majority of your decisions should move you toward innovation instead of toward cost-cutting. The team should seek to cut costs wherever a cost reduction will not interfere with their ability to drive innovation. This could be different for other teams. The exact ordering of your objectives will depend on the unique strategy of your organization, and the exact function of your team. The above example might be appropriate for the Research &

Development team at Apple Computer or the merchandising team at Target. Given the unique strategy of those organizations, cost-cutting should be in service of innovation and design. But the order of priorities might be completely reversed for the Supply Chain team at Target or for the regional manager's team at a discount grocer. In these cases, their efforts at innovation should focus on innovative ways to cut costs and improve efficiency.

6. The Pulse Chart

For leaders at the top of an organization, it is helpful to know how each of your teams or departments believes they are contributing to the organization's Decision Pulse. When stacked up next to each other, you might find that there is a disconnect between the way in which you thought a certain team would be contributing to driving the strategy and the way in which the team leader envisioned her team's role. For example, line managers who have their own profit and loss responsibilities might reasonably assume that "drive revenue growth" is their real Team Pulse, and treat "deliver service excellence" as sort of an after-thought that her team will attend to if and when the "real work" gets done. A Pulse Chart helps brings those miscommunications to light.

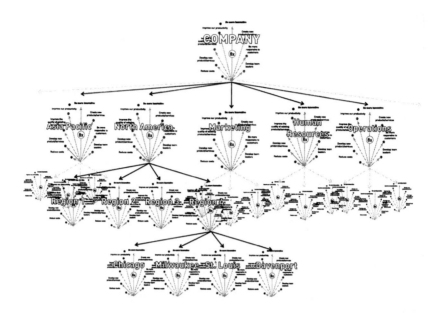

Think of the Pulse Chart as a strategic plan superimposed on a classic organization chart. Three advantages give the Pulse Chart a practical edge over the typical strategic plan. The first advantage is that it clarifies the primary strategic direction for teams throughout the organization while also leaving little room for managers and employees to be distracted by other directions that could arguably be "valuable," but strategically off point.

At the same time as it provides clarity about the strategic priorities, the Pulse Chart also leaves ample room for agility and adaptability. It makes clear the overall strategic direction, but does not try to spell out all of the operational details necessary to move in that direction. When the unexpected inevitably happens during the course of executing the strategy, managers and their teams have enough clear direction to make a good decision, but don't have to worry about "breaking from script." They can be flexible while still being directionally correct. The Pulse Chart enables people to behave strategically, rather than just passively receiving someone else's strategic orders.

Lastly, the Pulse Chart blends top down and bottom up strategy. Top management has the opportunity to set the overall direction. But the design of the Team Decision Pulse *process* that each team would go through empowers team members at all levels of the organization to actively participate in setting the direction for their team. Not only would the active participation increase psychological buy-in of the overall strategy, it also leaves plenty of room for each individual team to capture the nuances of their function, region, or skill set while still staying true to the strategic direction of the company as a whole.

The Pulse Chart could also be easily condensed into a snapshot version. Because the Team Pulse you already ranked and prioritize the direction during the Team Pulse discovery process, creating snapshots for printouts or slides during meetings and working sessions is fairly simple. If you are focusing on the organization as a whole, you can create a snapshot like the one below that reflects only the Decision Pulse for each team. Those in the meeting can be confident that all the other directions not listed stem directly from that team's Pulse. If it is necessary to drill down, then you can always revert to that team's Pulse diagram which lists all eight of their directions.

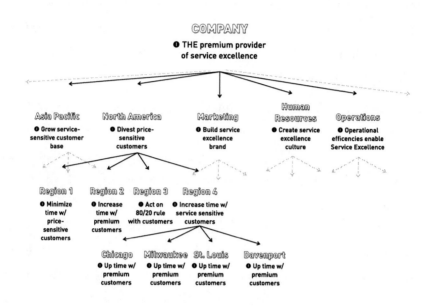

Getting clear about your Decision Pulse is the first critical element of strategic behavior. The next step is *using* it. In the following chapters, we'll explore how you and the rest of your team can use your Decision Pulse to make decisions faster and more strategically every day.

EXECUTIVE SUMMARY

- Decision Pulses aren't just for corporate executives or strategy consultants. Any individual or team who is concerned not just with creating a nice-looking strategy on paper, but in actually *executing*, should define a Pulse.

- The Team Pulse discovery process used with Randy Ross's HR department at G&K Services applies to teams of all sizes and works for teams of all sizes. The discovery process includes 5 steps:

   1. Who is your Customer?

   2. What is your Customer's ultimate strategic objective for the year?

   3. List all of the things your team does that adds value to your customer's strategic objective?

   4. Decide which of those valuable activities also make you unique in comparison to your peers and/or competitors.

   5. Decide which of those activities are both highly valuable and make you highly unique within your organization.

- Team Pulses should be clear, concise, and specific. Inspirational messages and clever verbiage are best reserved for speeches and vision statements.

CHAPTER FOUR

WHEN RATIONAL IS WRONG

"A great number of people think they are thinking when they are merely rearranging their prejudices."

--William James

Put yourself in Jim Donald's shoes. Or those of his predecessor Orin Smith. Or any other member of the Starbucks executive team circa 2007. A few years ago, you were handed control of an American icon—a darling of Wall Street for the past 16 years in a row. Your company literally has been a case study in business growth and successful global expansion. During your tenure, you increased earnings by 20% every year. Now a soft economy is leading many commentators—and comedians, for that matter—to suggest that your company might finally be reaching the point of market saturation. After all, how many Starbucks stores can realistically occupy a single city block? But Wall Street doesn't want to hear any excuses out of you, mister. You inherited the dream job. It is your responsibility to keep the machine running at top speed. You were put in place specifically to generate creative ways for the company to continue its meteoric rise—to keep on elevating the human spirit and the stock price at the same time. The economy is sliding toward free fall, and you already have so many stores operating that the new ones have begun to cannibalize the old ones. In breakfast sandwiches, you have found a product that observational data and market research both tell you your customers love. It is also a product that accounts for over 3% of your total annual sales. These are the facts you have going for you. The only dissenting voice is from the company's highly emotional founder. You are armed with reams of customer data. The founder's most compelling argument amounts to a question of "Where is the magic in burnt cheese?" *Really?* you think to yourself. *We are supposed to risk the future of a $10 billion enterprise, not to mention our jobs and the jobs of thousands of employees around the world, all because one of our most successful product lines doesn't "feel magical!?!"*

Based only on this information, if I asked you to decide whether Jim Donald or Howard Schultz was being more rational, who would you select? By now, you know that Schultz ultimately ended up selecting the right course of action within the context of their strategic direction. Objectively speaking, however, you would almost certainly have to conclude that Jim Donald's decision to *keep* the breakfast sandwiches was more rational than Schultz's decision to remove them. Donald's decision was based on clear, objective data as well as statistical facts and compelling anecdotes. That was the problem.

Similarly, in the example from Southwest Airlines, how could you argue that Tracy from Marketing's decision was not objectively rational? She was directly responding to the customer data at an airline that is "dedicated to the highest quality customer service." This is how good leaders in the Information Age should be making decisions, isn't it? When you get promoted into management in a corporation today, you might as well be issued a t-shirt that reads "Crazy for Analytics!"

Yet, the data in these cases did not tell the whole story. While analytics are invaluable within the context of a company's strategic direction, by themselves they are utterly useless, and even dangerous outside that context. They are simply numbers that have no practical value until your strategy assigns them meaning and value. The truth is that strategic behavior is always rational, but rational behavior is not always strategic.

This is also what Michael Porter was referring to when he claimed that a sound business strategy must require managers to occasionally make *suboptimal* choices. What Porter means is that, when viewed in isolation, choosing to do something like reject a paying customer segment, ignore customer requests, eliminate profitable business lines and products, or accept known inefficiencies in one part of the supply chain could be suboptimal for the situation, but highly rational for the overall strategy. If that paying customer segment does not align with the company's long-term strategy of low costs or of luxury services or that supply chain inefficiency enables the creation of a more distinct and sought after product then these "suboptimal" choices in isolation are still strategically optimal in the big picture. Strategically then, Howard Schultz's thinking was spot-on.

Detecting when these suboptimal choices are correct is difficult because of context. Psychologist Barry Schwartz argues that many allegedly "irrational" behaviors appear to be irrational only because they are taken out of their broader context. When we assess their logic, we look at them as isolated events that have no bearing on the decision maker's long-term future or past experiences. "Everything else is assumed to be fixed, including the decision maker's history, the shape of the paths that can be chosen from, and the future consequences of choosing one path," Schwartz argues. We could also add "the strategic direction of the decision maker" to his list of assumed fixed variables. Remember, the whole point of strategy is to do something that differentiates you, and fits your unique objectives. It makes sense then that one strategist's "irrational" decision could be another strategist's stroke of genius. The vast majority of modern researchers and practitioners of strategy and decision making have become so dogmatic in their belief in the power of data and the authority of objective analysis that it's starting to feel like a religion unto itself.

So I think it's worth taking a short trip back in time to see where this unquestioned worship at the altar of data and analytics first began. From there, we can more clearly define its boundaries and fully leverage its real strengths.

1. Rebounding Rationality

In the fall of 1939, a bookish 23-year old graduate student at the University of California at Berkeley named Herbert A. Simon took charge of an enormous research project. Together with three of his young colleagues, Simon shed new light on the connection between urban property taxes and municipal revenues in the San Francisco Metropolitan Area. Sensational reading, this study was not. If you cracked open your 1943 issue of the Quarterly Journal of Economics (it's probably on your coffee table right under that

US Weekly) and rated this report for excitement, it would score somewhere between a colonoscopy and a traffic jam.

But buried deep beneath the jargon and complex mathematical formulas in the article titled "Fiscal Aspects of Municipal Consolidation," Herbert Simon planted the seed of a very important idea. Simon observed that even if city managers were armed with identical information about taxes and revenues, they would often arrive at different conclusions. Each manager would necessarily focus on different pieces of information within the larger whole and reach a different decision than his colleagues. Simon concluded that people's ability to process information had limits. It was a simple yet revolutionary idea at the time. Whether you realize it or not, this idea significantly altered the trajectory of your life and mine, our society and the global economy. A few years after Fiscal Aspects was released to critical acclaim from upwards of a half-dozen reclusive economists, Simon published another book. In his now classic management text, *Administrative Behavior*, Simon gave his idea of limited information processing a name. He called it bounded rationality.

Simon argued that people and organizations, in order to function efficiently, must be willing to trade quality for speed when making decisions. Some choices must be made with the understanding that they might not be optimal, but are "good enough." He called this strategic pursuit of good enough "satisficing." For Simon, satisficing described what people were already doing (whether they knew it or not) and prescribed what we should be doing in light of our imperfections. In simple terms, Simon was saying, "*Sure, it would be great if we all had the time and processing power to analyze all the data before us. But, c'mon folks, let's be realistic. You don't have that kind of time or brain power. Pick your battles and start satisficing."*

According to the Nobel Committee in 1978, Simon was right. Around that same time, a burgeoning field of research — known by its street name, "behavioral economics" — picked up Simon's torch and proved just how bounded our rationality is. In experiment after experiment, behavioral economists showed that the everyday person's rationality was bounded, if not crippled, by scores of predictable biases and errors in judgment. Today, behavioral economists have pretty well shredded the age-old doctrine of the Efficient Markets Hypothesis which said that people always behave rationally, and that a collection of those rational people all making bets in the same marketplace will create an infallibly efficient system (pay no attention to the men behind the bubbles). Truth had finally conquered!

Sort of.

Simon's argument unleashed a powerful corollary. Inherent to the belief that boundaries represented imperfection was the idea that expanding those boundaries would move us closer to perfection —closer to our ideal state. Armed with that conclusion, Herbert Simon turned his full attention to computers and artificial intelligence models that were presumably much less bounded than the human mind. That is where his attention remained for the rest of his long, illustrious career. For the last half of the twentieth century, psychologists, economists and information technologists have passionately devoted themselves to creating systems and technologies that could free us from the limitations of our feeble human minds. All the laptops, smartphones, and iPads you'll see today in the coffee shop, at work, and in your living room demonstrate the enormous progress made so far. Perhaps the crowning achievement of the revolution came in February 2011 when IBM's voice-reading, pun-detecting Watson Supercomputer handily defeated two of Jeopardy's greatest champions with no assistance at all from a human being.

And yet here we are today. Despite the explosion of knowledge and technology aimed at enabling more rational analysis, people don't seem to be making better decisions. If we examine the state of our economy, our personal budgets, and our collective physical health, we could make a very compelling argument that people's general ability to make decisions is getting worse, not better. Unfortunately, the field of business strategy is no exception to this disturbing overall trend. Former CEO of Proctor & Gamble, A.G. Lafley and his colleagues argued in a 2012 Harvard Business Review article that: "strategic planners pride themselves on their rigor. Strategies are supposed to be driven by numbers and extensive analysis and uncontaminated by bias, judgment, or opinion. The larger the spreadsheets, the more confident an organization is in its process. All those numbers, all those analyses, feel scientific and in the modern world, 'scientific' equals good." Indeed that has been the primary takeaway from Simon's work on bounded rationality, which was really just an extension of the primary takeaway of the Age of Enlightenment beginning hundreds of years before. But as Lafley and his colleagues go on to argue, "conventional strategic planning is not actually scientific." The first critical step in the scientific method is the creation of hypotheses that can then be tested. If you have no hypotheses before you dive into a stack of data then you have nothing to test. You have nothing to validate or invalidate. All you have is a pile of numbers. By definition, that is an *unscientific* approach.

Strategic directions and the decisions that follow them are, and *should be*, a hypothesis that must be tested in the ever-changing world of real people. These hypotheses are as much the product of informed intuition as they are artificial intelligence. When strategic planners jump right into data gathering and spreadsheet-creation, they use information-gathering as a proxy for thinking.

2. No Gut, no glory?

If you've read anything in the last 10 years about how people make decisions, you have probably been confused. In his fascinating book, *Blink*, the author and thinker Malcolm Gladwell popularized the idea that many times our subconscious brain knows a lot more than our conscious brain can articulate. The lesson many people took away from *Blink* is that people should trust their gut instinct and ignore evidence and facts. At the same time, however, a whole slew of other books by behavioral economists—not to mention some of the other chapters in *Blink* itself—presented contrary evidence that suggested if we leave our choices up to gut instinct we expose ourselves to a litany of dangerous errors and harmful biases. Both arguments were compelling. So the conclusion that many people drew from this outpouring of information and advice is: I should trust my gut…except when I shouldn't.

Not surprisingly, one of the most common questions I've been asked by business leaders in recent years is "so is it better to trust your gut, or to rely on evidence?" In an attempt to be extra helpful, I answer them very clearly "yes." The truth is that both have a place in strategic thinking. When it comes to strategy, you must rely on informed instinct to hypothesize your strategic direction. You should then use data from purposely constructed tests to validate or invalidate that hypothesis. This is precisely the approach Angela Ahrendts took with Burberry's strategy. After her initial observation that none of her 60-some top executives wore Burberry trench coats, she led her team to survey the industry to see how they stacked up. Only then did Ahrendts dig into the data. "After brainstorming and formalizing our instincts, we commissioned a consulting firm to provide us with competitor benchmarking. Our instincts confirmed, we clearly saw the way forward: We would reinforce our heritage, our Britishness, by emphasizing and growing our core luxury products, innovating them and keeping them at the heart of everything we did." The important phrase there is "our instincts confirmed." Ahrendts knew all about the numbers. She hired a consulting firm to provide her with even more numbers. She used numbers to measure their progress and to track changes. But we should not forget that all of this began with a moment of insight. Her one observation at that first strategic planning meeting where of all the key leaders wore anything and everything *except* a Burberry trench coat is what led to the hypothesis that emphasizing Burberry's heritage would be strategically vital to realizing Burberry's potential.

Even IBM, the world's greatest champion of analytics understands the limitations of data. At the time of this writing, Ginni Rometty is still the CEO of IBM and Watson the Supercomputer has yet to be offered a position anywhere on IBM's leadership team.

Take for example uniform and facilities services company we looked at in the last chapter, G&K Services. After reviewing a number of competitive factors, CEO Doug Milroy and his team discovered that they already had an edge over competitors in the area of customer satisfaction. This in itself was not a hunch. Rather it was a fact according to a commonly used customer satisfaction measure. Relative to their competitors, G&K Services scored higher than everyone else in the industry. But this was just one piece of data. It still required real people at G&K Services to decide how that data would change their strategy. High customer satisfaction does not always equate to profitability. Precisely how much higher than competitors would it need to be to create a measurable advantage? Would the company be better served by working to lower their prices and become more efficient with their logistics? If they did end up deciding to compete on customer satisfaction, how would that change their current strategy? Could they realistically make the rest of their activities fit with that new strategy? Ultimately they decided that they would make themselves the "THE provider of Service Excellence" in their industry segment. Could they be absolutely certain that this would take them to the land of milk and honey? Of course not. The future is inherently uncertain, and that's why strategic planning and future predictions remain a very human endeavor. But just *how uncertain* is still often misunderstood.

3. The Real World of Radical Uncertainty

Imagine that I put an opaque jar in front you. It has 50 red balls in it and 50 black balls in it. Your job is to pull out a red ball. If you stick your hand in this jar, you can't be certain whether you'll get a red ball or a black ball. That's what makes the outcome uncertain. But you do know that you have a 50% chance of getting a red ball and a 50% chance of getting a black ball. It's like a roulette wheel. This jar is an example of basic uncertainty, which is how most of us tend to think of the future. We don't know exactly what is going to happen, but being the astute, rational beings we are, we do know that determining the probabilities of different outcomes is what the smartest people would do. In this world of uncertainty, we should make our decisions based on which choice has the highest probably of giving us our desired outcome. That used to be really hard to do given the computational challenges required. But now we have computers and software packages who can calculate this stuff with a few strokes of the keyboard.

If you approach your decisions in this way, you are implicitly making two vital assumptions. The first is that your assessment of the probabilities can be accurately determined by you or by your computer. The second assumption is that all of the relevant variables remain static and unchanging between the time you make the decision and the time the outcome actually occurs. Unfortunately, this approach is a poor representation of reality.

Our world operates much closer to the scenario surrounding a second jar. This other jar has balls in it. Some of the balls are red and some of them are black. But you have no idea how many there are in total, let alone how many red balls there are in comparison to the black balls. You could guess at the probabilities, but that would be all it is—a wild guess. Until you dig in and start pulling some of the balls out, you will have no way of coming up with even a reasonable estimate of the probabilities, and about whether the balls are mostly red, mostly black or an even split. University of Chicago economist Frank Knight first pointed out this distinction in 1921. Knight concluded that the most commonly accepted ways of measuring uncertainty were actually probabilistic calculations of risk, which is fine if you have enough information about the probabilities. But in the real world where individual enterprises seek to prosper, not nearly enough of the situational probabilities can be known in advance about their specific situation to make even a reasonably certain calculation ahead of time.

You can think of it this way: Actuaries at insurance companies employ all sorts of data to predict how people will behave. They are able to accurately estimate the probability that 42-year old motorcycle-riding females who do not smoke and live in a coastal metropolitan area will get into a motorcycle accident. This is a risk probability calculation based on averages from a huge sample of past data from women who meet these criteria. But that is nowhere near the same complexity and level of uncertainty involved in a strategic decision that by its very nature is unique and novel. A strategic decision would be much more like this: A specific woman named Jane Robbins is 42 and likes to ride motorcycles in San Francisco, and she is contemplating whether or not it will be a good career move to accept a job transfer to Singapore. You know a lot of data about Jane, but most of it is useless for predicting the specific outcome of Jane's potential move. You would first have to calculate how Jane defines "good career move" and what would be the cost of staying where she is, or of examining transfers to Chicago or Miami. In comparison to the motorcycle accidents question, we have virtually no data about women in Jane's exact demographic and industry and job level with the same personal preferences, behavioral patterns, relationship ties, strengths, weaknesses, goals and surrounding environmental characteristics who also moved to Singapore and whether or not it was a "good career move" for them. In other words, existing past data is useless here. It would be like Apple Computer trying to determine whether introducing the iPad was a smart thing to do by looking at historical sales trends of technology companies introducing a new hardware. The differences are too numerous to count. Even if we did have all of the relevant data, Jane doesn't really care whether this could be a good career move for 57.4% of women *like* her. She is not interested in balancing the mean for the rest of her demographic in the same way Apple Computer doesn't really care about whether only 31% of technology companies have historically succeeded with new product launches. They weren't Apple. They weren't iPads. None of them launched the same product on the same day in the same way in the same stores targeting the same customers with the same competitive landscape.

So what can we conclude about how to think and behave strategically in this radically uncertain world?

Until you step into the situation by making your initial decision, much of the information you will need to be successful is not just uncertain, it is *unknowable*. That means data will not give you the answer ahead of time. You need to act on the information you have while fully understanding that you don't have nearly all of the relevant information. Your first Decision Pulse is itself a hypothesis generated by your informed intuition and debate among your team members. As such, it requires targeted testing and data gathering to validate or invalidate the unique circumstances. On the other hand, simply knowing your Decision Pulse will not automatically guarantee that you think rationally about how your options align with your Pulse in the moment. You cannot make a strategically rational decision without knowing what your Decision Pulse is. However, just knowing your Decision Pulse and acting in alignment with your Pulse during the hustle and bustle of your day are two different things. In other words, knowing your decision pulse is necessary but not sufficient for strategic behavior. Simon and his intellectual heirs are correct in their claim that sometimes we let our emotions and irrational impulses lead us to do things we wish we hadn't. We hire people who were clearly poor candidates right from the start. We buy things we regret. We pursue flawed strategies, investing in products and businesses that make little sense, strategically or otherwise. That is why we need to build a simple, yet effective logic-checker into our daily decision routine. That is the topic of the next chapter.

EXECUTIVE SUMMARY

- *strategic behavior is always rational, but rational behavior is not always strategic.*

- Herbert Simon correctly asserted that human beings have "bounded rationality". Although computers are less bounded in their rationality, they cannot eliminate uncertainty.

- Strategic behavior is still a very human activity. Even IBM's Watson supercomputer doesn't get to make IBM's strategic decisions.

- Decisions will always be characterized a future that is radically uncertain, much like the opaque jar with a bunch of colored balls in it, some of which are red and some are black. We can guess the probabilities, but even probability estimates will be severely limited.

- Gut instinct is not the final answer. Our intuition has very real flaws. It is however, a necessary and vital part of our functioning.

- Every decision is a hypothesis within a mini-experiment. The hypothesis is not the final conclusion, but it is the essential first step toward revealing some truth about the situation.

CHAPTER FIVE

CONSULT THE ANTI-YOU

"Chance favors the prepared mind."

--Louis Pasteur

One hot July afternoon, I made a terrible decision.

I vividly remember the moments leading up to it. There I was, sitting behind the wheel of a brand new 31-foot Coachmen Leprechaun. My flip-flops rested near the pedals that commanded an enormous Ford V-10 engine. Directly behind me were nearly 10 yards' worth of home-on-the-road living quarters, complete with a flat screen TV, stainless steel kitchen appliances, a three-quarter bathroom, central air and a queen-size bed. Riding shotgun was a very eager salesman wearing a sweaty, half-tucked polo shirt, and a severe case of bedhead, even though it was late afternoon. Moments later, this fellow and I would be shaking hands and signing papers.

On the drive home that day, a number of thoughts raced through my mind. *What exciting destination would my wife and our brand new son visit first? Since the RV comfortably sleeps eight passengers, who would join us on that excursion? What will my wife say when she sees me drive up in this puppy?* Shortly after that last question I took a hard right away from mindless exhilaration and toward palpable panic. *Good lord, what did I just do?* I eventually concluded that in the entire history of decision-making, buying this RV ranked right up there with Neville Chamberlin's choice to appease the Nazis and Eve deciding to nibble on that apple in the Garden of Eden.

Even though I had not yet given a name to the concept that became the Decision Pulse, I did have a fairly good sense at the time that the strategic direction for my life was Freedom. And this was part of the problem.

Sometimes even if we have a clear definition of our strategic direction, our emotions and impulses can cloud our judgment and send us away from our strategic direction. In a matter of three months, my wife and I exposed ourselves to some of the most categorically stressful changes people endure throughout the course of a well-lived life. We moved across country from San Diego to Minneapolis. One month after that we bought our first home. One month after that, our first child was born. To say this was a stressful time would be the understatement of the year. In my overwhelmed state of mind, buying an RV seemed like a perfect way to move me in the strategic direction of freedom. After all what spells "freedom" more than cruising down the open road with everything I need stacked up on two axles? Needless to say that the storage, the maintenance, the comically low gas mileage, and virtually every other aspect of that motorhome did nothing but add obligation and restriction to my life—the exact opposite of freedom.

The real error in this case is that I jumped directly from checking my Decision Pulse to making the decision. I neglected the second vital step in the strategic decision process: Consult an anti-you.

1. Good Decisions Come From Experience

Two years later when I sold the RV (creating a sizable tax shelter for the year, thank you very much) my wife, my brother, my parents, and a long line of friends were all too happy to tell me that they couldn't believe I made the purchase decision in the first place. Where was this great advice two years ago, I wondered.

I think we can draw two lessons from this experience. The first lesson is that sometimes we mess up. Those screw-ups are a normal, healthy part of sharpening our judgment. The 13th century Turkish sage named Nasreddin put this quite nicely in a lesson to one of his protégés.

"Master, where do good decisions come from?" the younger man asked.

"Good decisions come from experience," Nasreddin replied.

They rode a few steps further when the younger man asked him another question. "Master, where does experience come from?

After thinking for a moment Nasreddin answered. "Experience comes from bad decisions."

My ill-fated motorhome purchase added an important layer of depth to my understanding of how my Decision Pulse fares under real world conditions. In this case, I learned that one entire category of alternatives could be ruled out from consideration in future personal decisions. What I had previously regarded as symbols of a certain kind of freedom (financial)—recreational vehicles, boats, second homes, etc.—did not actually appeal at all to *my* definition of freedom. For me, this turned out to be a strategically *irrational* choice. But this was a variation of the scientific method that A.G. Lafley suggests for creating winning business strategies. It starts by creating hypotheses, and then running tests on these hypotheses to either validate or invalidate them in real world circumstances. This test did not change my Decision Pulse. It sharpened my understanding of it, and strengthened my relationship with it.

That being said, I still wish I had not purchased the motorhome. There could have been a much less expensive way to learn this lesson. As leaders of organizations, teams, or households we can't afford to learn too many of these costly lessons without bankrupting ourselves or losing our jobs.

The good news is that the science of decision-making has come a long way in recent years. Psychologists and behavioral economists have discovered some simple measures we can take to minimize the damage of our irrational slips, without paralyzing ourselves by hesitation, analysis, and indecision. In an excellent summary, Katherine Milkman of the Wharton School lists techniques which include taking an outsider's perspective; asking a genuine outsider for their input; and considering the opposite outcome; among others. The catch-all phrase I use for these techniques is "consult the anti-you." The point of consulting the anti-you is to apply some method for stepping outside of your bounded frame of reference to see the situation from a new angle. By consulting the Anti-You, you are still operating on the premise that good decisions come from experience. Only now you are not limiting yourself to your own personal experience. You are tapping into someone else's experience before making a costly error. Not to minimize the wisdom and experience of my fellow management consultants and executive coaches, but at least half of the value consultants provide to their clients derives as much from our inherently external point of view as it does from any accumulated expertise or innate brilliance. (Present company excluded, of course).

In our personal lives this can be as simple as calling up a friend. In a more professional context, the same basic principle applies but it can take on different forms. The following are two simple, yet effective variations of consulting the anti-you in an organizational context.

2. The Foresight Bias Activity

The first big decision Randy Ross's team at G&K Services had to make after deciding on their Decision Pulse was how to realign their department to fit the strategic direction. We broke up his core leadership team into four groups. Each group had two weeks to come up with a proposed structure that would be most conducive to creating a "service excellence brand that was recognized and sought after." When we returned for the next working session, we began like always by reiterating the Decision Pulse for this particular department realignment project: "creating a new department structure that will make G&K's Service Excellence brand recognized and sought after." After discussing the various models, the team decided on one model that would serve as the first iteration. Since the results of this project affected every department in the company, a long line of Anti-You's in the form of executives and line managers from other departments were waiting in the wings to offer their opinions. In fact, we had called on some of these internal experts already to do exactly that during the team's initial Team Pulse discovery process. But because this was a high visibility project within the company, Ross knew that it would be risky to push out a half-baked idea that was deemed completely off the mark, even if he made it clear that this was only a "rough draft" of the new design. It could still severely damage the project's credibility going forward. On the one hand, they already had a built-in Anti-You in me, the outside consultant. But we also wanted the group to engage in another low-risk version of consulting the Anti-You.

The foresight bias activity allows you take advantage of that uniquely human ability to imagine alternative futures. In their small groups the team wrote a response to two scenarios.

Scenario 1:

Imagine it is December 31 and the project has been a whopping success. As a result of the realignment, people at all levels of the company take pride in this culture where every single person clearly understands how their job connects to the Customer Promise and demonstrates those behaviors every day. Your friend Sarah is embarking on a similar project at her company and she is dying to know how you pulled this off. Explain to Sarah what parts of the proposed model were the most critical to making your Service Excellence brand recognized and sought after.

Scenario 2:

Imagine it is December 31 and the project has been a horrible disaster. As a result of the realignment, the Service Excellence culture has become a punch line for the company's employees. Nobody outside of the corporate office even knows that there is a Customer Promise, let alone demonstrates the behaviors. Your friend Sam is embarking on a similar project at his company. Sam is dying to know how to avoid the same disaster. Explain to Sam what parts of the proposed model doomed the model.

Decision expert Gary Klein uses a similar version of this technique called the "premortem" analysis (as opposed to a postmortem). As Klein describes it, this technique is a "sneaky way to get people to do contrarian, devil's advocate thinking without encountering emotional resistance....The logic is that instead of showing people that you are smart because you can come up with a good plan, you show you're smart by thinking of insightful reasons why this project might go south."

After the group at G&K did this activity, it became apparent that their decision would likely generate significant pushback from other leaders in the organization. But it truly was best way forward for the team and the company. So, this insight didn't materially change the decision itself, but it did change their approach to implementing the decision. That is one of the biggest advantages of the foresight activity. Decisions do not exist in a vacuum. The "right" decision can go terribly wrong during the execution of that decision. Similarly, a relatively poor decision can be corrected by good follow-up decisions that adapt well to the circumstances. The foresight activity may not change your decision, but it enables you to alter the execution of that decision to avoid derailers and capitalize on momentum-builders.

3. The Prouty Red Team

A few years ago, David Mortenson, the executive vice president of Mortenson Construction, stared across the table at four strangers. At the time, the economy was starting to slump and taking the construction industry down with it. Residential building had nearly screeched to a halt and commercial building wasn't far behind. And now, Mr. Mortenson and his executive team found themselves presenting the strategy for their company's future to this small group of visitors.

They weren't bankers. They weren't customers. They weren't board members. They were the Red Team. Four months prior to that day, Mortenson Construction had called in a boutique strategy consulting firm that I work with called The Prouty Project. They wanted the Prouty consultants to help them reimagine what Mortenson Construction could do to maintain their competitive advantage in the brave new world that was fast approaching. After a few weeks Mortenson's management team made a breakthrough.

"The biggest epiphany for us was realizing that customers *assume* on-time and under-budget building projects," Mortenson said. That meant that "on-time" and "under-budget" was not a valid differentiator. After months of deliberation they concluded that in order to stay ahead of the competition, they would need to deliver an exceptional experience, not an expected one. They had developed a hypothesis about what that experience would look like, and how to deliver it. But at the moment, it was just that—a hypothesis. They had to ask themselves "Was this new direction correct for us?"

Although this is exactly the right question to ask when faced with an uncertain future, if not managed properly this question can create a toxic case of analysis paralysis. That's because we've invoked the primal, impulsive part of our brain that is always there to remind us that taking this next step could lead us into the jaws of the hungry bear we know as Failure. While under the spell of this last-minute logic, our rational faculties are overpowered by our impulses. Our brains have an extremely well-designed triage system designed first and foremost for survival. When we sense something that feels like a threat, every system in our body that is not immediately necessary to get ourselves out of harm's way gets sent to the waiting area. It is designed to prevent us from doing any complicated cost-benefit analyses before jumping out of the way of an oncoming car or running away from the rabid dog. But it's also why we don't always think clearly before taking that first step into a new and uncertain future. In these moments, our impulses once again revert back to their most basic goal—survival now, not prosperity in the future. They are guided by emotional memories of past failures and personal biases that we've accumulated over a lifetime of experience, which makes them a very strong force.

This is where the Prouty Red Team comes into play. The Prouty Red Team is a small group of executives and thought leaders from outside the client's industry that can provide a truly external voice at the end of a strategic planning process. They come from very different worlds so they have accumulated a very different set of "common knowledge" than the client team. They also have the added advantage of not being privy to the discussions that led to the current strategic plan so they have no emotional attachment to one course of action versus another. The Red Team (or the Anti-You's) not only shed light on some of the real risks lurking in the shadows of our mind, they also help leaders like Mortenson's senior team confidently answer that important question *Is this direction right for us?*

To be clear, a strong track record of success and collective experience has given the Mortenson team plenty of confidence. Yet, even the boldest leaders have moments of self-doubt — not so much about the quality of their judgment — but about which variables they might not be able to see or control. The Anti-You(s) help neutralize that doubt. Ultimately, this empowers management to implement their new strategy with clarity and confidence. Four years later, in spite of the economic slump, Mortenson Construction has increased their lead over competitors, and their business has expanded despite the fact that commercial construction is down over 40%. Mortenson's growth over the past four years is no doubt due to a solid strategy and skilled execution. But we should never forget that behind every brilliant strategic execution at Mortenson Construction or anywhere else, one leader or leadership team made a decision to choose a single course of action. Anti-You's like the Red Team help insure that your team is not only clear about the strategic direction, but that they are choosing to pursue a course that aligns with that direction.

EXECUTIVE SUMMARY

- "Good decisions come from experience…Experience comes from bad decisions." --Nasreddin

- Every decision should incorporate a simple, yet effective logic-check.

- Leaping directly from checking your decision pulse to making a decision without consulting an anti-you in between, might just make you the proud (and regretful) owner of a motorhome.

- In an organizational context, two variations on consulting an Anti-You are highly effective:

1. The Foresight Bias Activity takes advantage of our 20/20 hindsight…ahead of time by imagining alternate futures and explaining how we got there.

2. The Prouty Red Team involves bringing in a team of true outsiders with no background in your business or your situation to kick the tires on your strategy.

CHAPTER SIX

DO'S AND DON'TS

"In real life, strategy is actually very straightforward. You pick a general direction and implement like Hell."

--Jack Welch

It is time to dive deeper into the third and final part of the Know-Think-Do framework. The Know part of the framework was about clarifying your Decision Pulse. The Think part of the framework is about analyzing which options align best with your Decision Pulse. Both the Know and Think parts of the framework are about strategic thinking. But as we learned in the General Mills research, knowing your strategic direction and thinking strategically about that direction is not enough. To be effective, you also have to *Do* something with all of those thoughts. You have to finish the job. That's why the third part of the framework is Do. Ironically, making the decision is the most overlooked step in the decision process. Most often we place the emphasis almost entirely on the Think step. That is important but it is only effective when it is sandwiched between knowing the strategic direction and taking action based on our thoughts.

The Do step is where most people stumble. To illustrate why, imagine for a second that you were Bill Mott. By way of Doc Brown's DeLorean or some other run-of-the-mill time machine, you are thrust back in time and landed in Bill Mott's hiking boots in the summer of 1988. There you are humming along to Whitney Houston in her prime getting *so emotional* on the boom box in your office (you are a very hip 80 years old). Right about the time Whitney hits her first crescendo, you receive a call. On the other end of the line is the head ranger at Yellowstone telling you about a few small fires that have ignited recently in the park.

What will you do?

On the one hand, you know that the best available information suggests that the future health of Yellowstone National Park—the jewel in the crown of the U.S. National Park Service—will be best served by letting the fire burn. Of course, all you have to base your decision on is a theory about controlled burning. Even though you have tried to educate everyone from politicians to media members about the science behind this theory, your words have fallen on deaf ears. And you've already gone rounds over a wolf reintroduction program with an outspoken cadre of U.S. congressmen in that region led by a powerful representative from Wyoming named Richard "Dick" Cheney. It's going to be a fight.

On the other hand, you are Bill Mott. You have been a nature-lover all of your life. If you opt to ignore the current knowledge and suppress the fire, you won't have to sit idly by while hundreds of thousands of perfectly healthy trees, shrubs, and other lush vegetation are devoured by flames. You will be applauded by both the media, as well as your indirect bosses at the U.S. Congress and their ranching and farming constituencies in Wyoming and Montana. In the eyes of the public who is woefully unaware of how wildfires act like nature's housekeeper, you might even become the hero of the day.

So there it is. If you put out the fires you will save millions of trees from burning but prevent the forest from flourishing. If you let the fires burn you will lose millions of trees and be roundly criticized by uninformed commentators, but you will be saving the forest.

What would you decide?

1. Why Quitting Hurts

If the mere act of imagining yourself in this kind of tradeoff situation is making your palms sweat and your cheeks flush, you're not alone. According to studies conducted by researcher Mary Frances Luce and her colleagues at Duke University's Fuqua School of Business, if we could peer into your psyche right now I would likely find you about as comfortable as you would be in the waiting room before an anesthesia-free root canal. Even though this is only a hypothetical scenario, you probably just became slightly more pessimistic about your future. Your self-esteem just dropped a few notches and you might have even slipped into a mild temporary depression. On a scale of 1 to 10 where 10 is your bliss-filled wedding day and 1 is an IRS audit, the pleasure center of your brain is giving this experience about a 2...tops. The point is that making the right tradeoff—choosing to quit on the right things, is less a logic problem. It is an emotional problem. Logic can't help you anymore. It is you versus your emotions.

So how is all of this emotional strife likely to make you respond? Chances are you will do anything you can to avoid making the decision altogether. You might "delegate" the decision to the head ranger at Yellowstone. Maybe you recall some cool new idea about finding "win-win" solutions (remember it's only 1988, so Stephen Covey has not yet taken that idea mainstream). You might take a wait-and-see approach while you pray for a freak inland hurricane to wash away your conundrum. Or perhaps you would delay the decision a bit longer so you could call on some reputable experts to tell you what you already know?

The truth is that most decisions have no universally "wrong" answer or "right" answer. They have no win-win solution. Choosing x necessarily means sacrificing the benefits of y, and vice-versa. No amount of predictive forecasting, information gathering, elegant algorithms, off-site retreats, or mysterious powers of intuition will save all the trees *and* protect the health of the forest for future generations. In order to select one option you must quit on all the others. In reality, this is not an anomaly or a one-off type of scenario. Quitting other options is quite literally what deciding is all about.

Think about these words: homicide, suicide, genocide, fratricide. The Latin root of all those words is *cide* which means "to kill" or "to cut." Do you know what other English word shares the Latin root of *cide*? You guessed it: decide. I think the Ancient Romans understood something fundamental about the nature of deciding that our modern culture has either forgotten or chosen to ignore due to its uncomfortable reality. Decisions necessarily involve the death of other options. The reason why we are indecisive in our personal life or why we execute plans at work in a "ready, aim, aim, aim…" manner is not because we are unclear about what we want. It is because we have not come to terms with the fact that we must quit the other options we *also* want.

In fact, modern neuroscience confirms what the Ancient Romans already knew. In recent years, scientists have discovered that "free will" doesn't accurately describe the process a normal human brain uses to make decisions. When we are presented with a choice, the older, emotional center of our brains instantly and automatically floods the rational part of the brain with possible responses. When we see a certain number pop up on our caller ID, we are immediately presented with an option to answer it, ignore it until it goes to voicemail, actively decline it so the phone stops ringing, and/or send a text message to person whose call we are about to screen. The higher-order part of our brain that distinguishes humans from most other species then goes to work examining the implications of each choice and *eliminating* all of the response options except for the one we eventually select. In this regard, people with impulse control disorders who constantly do things they regret actually have more free will than the average well-adjusted adult. That is the problem. They struggle to lead happy, productive lives not because they lack free will, but because they lack free *won't*. They have trouble killing all of the other options they get an urge to act on and so they wind up bouncing from one activity to another without ever getting where they want to go.

2. Be a Decider

As Tim Judge's studies about people's inherent beliefs about their ability to deal with the events in their lives revealed, some people are innately more decisive than others. Although personality traits are hard to change, behaviors are more susceptible to influence. The good news is that the act of making a decision is a behavior, and not a trait. Renowned social scientist James March has found that our sense of identity exerts a powerful impact on our behavior. We are more or less likely to behave in a certain way depending on whether or not we believe that "someone like me" would do x or do y.

A few years ago, researchers at the University of Missouri found there was an enormous gap in goal achievement between people who merely wrote down a goal and those who rewrote their goal as an identity statement. For example instead of saying "my goal is to run three times a week" they would write down "I am a runner." A goal is simply something we do—it's a task we want to accomplish. An identity is more robust because it is about who we are regardless of external circumstances. Come rain, sleet, or snow, runners run. If you merely set a goal to run, it is far too easy to make excuses for why today won't work to run. "Tomorrow is the day!" we'll assure ourselves. Then we make a different excuse tomorrow and the next day, and the next.

Of course, the trick to making this all work is desire. You have to *want* to be a decider for your own reasons. If you don't believe that you will be better off in the areas you care most about by being more decisive, then you will not adopt a decisive identity. But I hope that by now you have seen how much decisiveness can accelerate your pursuit of personal and professional excellence.

The identity piece is especially important with regard to decisions simply because of the sheer volume of choices we must make every day. Unlike jogging three times a week, or conducting a staff meeting once a month, we make decisions every day. Sheena Iyengar at Columbia University has found that the typical American makes an average of 70 decisions every day. To prevent insanity, we have to make most of these decisions more or less automatically. If our default setting (i.e. our identity) is decisive instead of indecisive, then our automatic response will likely be a decisive one.

As is so often the case with decisions, one indisputably right answer never clearly emerges. Each option presents its own set of unique costs and benefits. That means you end up with a small handful of equally attractive or unattractive options—all of which could reasonably align with your decision pulse, and make rational strategic sense. There is simply no way to know which of those good options is "best", or which of the unpleasant options is necessary. As a leader, you have to make the decision even in the face of incomplete information or an imperfect set of choices. That is precisely why this is the point in the decision process where most otherwise good teams and leaders stop short of greatness. The thinking is that more data, more time, more discussion, and more second opinions will somehow enable you to predict the future and reveal a clear and indisputable right answer. At the moment of truth, it is far too easy for an individual decision-maker, let alone a team of decision makers to get sucked into analysis paralysis. I counsel my clients to remember that the purpose of a decision is not to find the perfect option, but to move you to the next decision. (The shorthand for that little nugget of wisdom is "next, not best.") I do not advocate lazy or shoddy thinking habits. But I am trying to get my clients to embrace the inherent uncertainty of the world in which they must operate successfully every day. That uncertainty can never be an excuse for inaction or the failure to *do* something.

All that being said, however, this book is as much about *not* doing as it is doing. Paradoxically, the secret to succeeding in the "Do" part of the Know-Think-Do framework comes mostly from focusing attention on what you are going to *quit* doing.

3. Non-Action Plan

As both a writer and a business consultant I often find myself straddling two worlds. So I always delight when lessons in one world transfer to the other. Aspiring writers who want to polish their work are often advised to "murdering their darlings." A "darling" is any piece of writing—a clever word play, a fascinating back story, a catchy phrase—that the writer really loves, but that sticks out in the overall narrative. In other words, a darling is a legitimately good piece of writing by all standards of objective rationality, but is out of place by the standards of strategic rationality. Darlings are to a compelling narrative what breakfast sandwiches were to Starbucks circa spring 2008. Although it stings, good writers force themselves to ruthlessly edit out those zingers and clever one-liners that just don't fit with the overall story, and distract the reader from digesting the story's main message. I've found this same truth so enormously powerful in teams and organizations that I've operationalized it for my clients in the form of a Non-Action Plan.

Earlier in my career, I would come in to an organization and help a team try to get focused by figuring out what they really wanted to accomplish. We would have a spirited debate of the kind that high-functioning teams are supposed to have before eventually arriving at a common goal to focus on and rally around. We would then create a nice, tight action plan about how to achieve this goal. Then the meeting would adjourn. Everyone would leave. And weeks later… nothing would get accomplished. Why? More often than not, the failure was not due to subtle unspoken resistance, siloed thinking, turf wars, or the other usual suspects. Indeed, with the help of wiser consultants and leaders than myself I started going out of my way to help all the team members around the room determine for themselves exactly how achieving that team objective would not only benefit the team, but also their individual careers. They were motivated by the spirit of teamwork and by self-interest, and…the results didn't change. My failure was in not asking the teams to specifically name the pet projects and previous priorities that would likely distract them in the coming weeks. We had created a fantastic Action Plan, but we failed to create a Non-Action Plan.

Deciding what you want to do only gets you half way to your desired destination. Deciding and explicitly stating what else you are not going to do is what gets you the rest of the way. Most successful leaders implicitly recognize this reality, but only a very select few put this truth into action with dogged consistency week after week. Far too often, this vital truth is a mere afterthought in discussions of good decision making and effective execution. The reasoning goes something like this: "if we just get really clear about what we want, then all the other stuff will naturally evaporate from our consciousness." The logic sounds good, but reality refutes it.

In a series of experiments New York University psychologist Peter Gollwitzer tested how likely people would be distracted based on the kind of reminder they used to stick to their plan. One group used a positive reminder such as "whenever the distraction arises, I will increase my efforts at hand!" The other group used a slightly different reminder that suggested "whenever the distraction arises, I will ignore it!" One phrase reminded people to stay focused on the desired goal, while the other reminded them to ignore the distraction. That subtle wording difference exerted a significant impact on how successfully people fended off distraction and remained focus.

Ignoring distractions is more effective than simply trying to stay focused. Gollwitzer believes the differing results have to do with the amount of mental effort required. Even overachievers have a finite amount of mental capacity. Our brains are designed to make us "cognitive misers." Wherever possible, our brains will conserve energy by taking shortcuts and "staying focused" requires lots of mental energy. To be sure, ignoring a distraction takes some effort, but not as much effort as trying to double up our focus when a distraction appears.

I even apply this technique at a very micro level. For example, I tend to be far more productive early in the morning than I am later in the day. This is especially true when I need to write something. Typically, I get more writing done between the hours of 5 a.m. and 8 a.m. than I could between 9 a.m. and 5 p.m. After mid-morning my muse clocks out for the day and takes all my creative juices with her. So I've come to regard these early morning hours as both precious and scarce. If I don't use them wisely, it's like losing a whole day. However, when I'm not writing a book, the first thing I typically do in the morning is fire up my laptop and check my email. That is a very hard habit to break when I need to slip back into writing mode. I've found that blocking out my calendar for those hours with an event title that says "Write 500 words" is often not enough to stop my habitual urge to check my email, even though that event comes with a handy automatic reminder that pops up on both my phone and my computer. What begins as a "quick check-in" turns into hours of emails and research on cool new ideas I dreamt up the night before. Neither activity is bad per se…unless you have a book deadline to meet. So now my event reminder reads like this "NO EMAIL, STUPID!! Write 500 words!" Not exactly the early morning self-affirmation you might like, but self-denigration works pretty well for me. Either way, the same premise applies. If you don't clearly list probable distractions like pet projects and outdated priorities, you are effectively removing the teeth from your decision about what to focus on. The likely result is that a whole team of talented, well-meaning people will go on their merry way only to spend the next month, quarter, or year getting sucked into the perfectly rational pursuit of projects that are no longer strategic priorities.

A non-action plan requires the team to actively call out all of those previous priorities, tempting goals, and other possible objectives that might add value but don't align with your strategy. I typically recommend a 3-6 month timeframe for the Non-Action Plan. That means all the projects and objectives you place on the non-action plan do not disappear forever. It just means you are agreeing to put them on the back-burner for the designated time period. Similarly, my "NO EMAIL, STUPID!!" reminder doesn't mean I will never again check my email. I will indeed check email later that same morning. Similarly, your non-action plan is not so much a graveyard as it a holding pen for projects whose time to shine has not yet come.

4. Process, Personality and Pressure

So far, our journey has been devoted almost exclusively to the Know-Think-Do framework for strategic behavior. That's because knowing your strategic direction; thinking in a strategically rational way about your options; and doing what it takes to bring that strategy to life are the key ingredients in the strategic behavior recipe. However, three other forces play a significant role in a leader, a team, or an organization's ability to behave strategically on a regular basis. To help ourselves, our teams, and our organizations behave strategically we must also learn how to leverage the forces of process, pressure, and personality. We need to train ourselves to use the three-step *process* every time we make a decision, big or small, every day. We also have to account for the way our *personality* and natural behavior patterns will influence our approach and the approach of our team members when trying to put that process into action. Lastly, we have to understand how the *pressures* from the surrounding environment influence our ability to behave strategically. While these forces have the most influence on Doing—the actual delivery of decisive action—they also play a role during the Know and Think phases as well.

In the next three chapters we will turn our attention to those forces. We will examine how the Civil War was—or at least *should have been*—won with a few hundred thousand lives to spare; what the difference is between ignorant simplicity and enlightened simplicity; how environmental pressures could save our forests and transform our leaders; and how good teams come together to be strategically decisive.

EXECUTIVE SUMMARY

- After you have made sure to check your Decision Pulse (Know), and tested your logic by consulting an anti-you (Think), you have only one step left to take; you have to *Do* something. No decision process is ever complete without action.

- Tough decisions almost always require a tradeoff where there is no objectively "best" answer. This is where the problem becomes less of a thinking problem, and more of an emotional problem.

- *Free won't* means the higher-order parts of our brains are naturally designed for eliminating options.

- "I am a decider" is a powerful way to reshape your approach to decisions. Decisiveness is a behavior pattern that anyone can learn. Whether or not you start to behave more decisively depends a lot on whether or not you adopt a decider's identity.

- A Non-Action Plan is an effective way to call out likely distractions that get in the way of executing a decision.

CHAPTER SEVEN

PROCESS: ENLIGHTENED SIMPLICITY & THE ADVANTAGE OF TIME

"A good plan, violently executed now, is better than a perfect plan next week."

--General George S. Patton

It was a crisp early spring day in 1862 when a handsome, young general marched nearly 150,000 soldiers toward the Potomac River. Crowds of civilian onlookers could not help but be impressed by the well-heeled troops as they paraded across the soggy ground away from their massive Washington D.C. camp site in high spirits and sporty, new uniforms. After climbing aboard the more than 400 ships transporting them to southern Virginia, the charismatic young general assured his men that "my fate is linked with yours…I am to watch over you as a parent over his children, and you know that your General loves you from the depths of his heart."

Despite his heartfelt address and his obvious affection for his men, General George McClellan was no weakling. Eight months before on July 27, 1861, Abraham Lincoln granted McClellan command of the Union Army's largest fighting force. When McClellan arrived in Washington the troops were disorganized and demoralized. Within days the brilliant "young Napoleon" was shaping up the entire army. His confidence was contagious. He inspired his soldiers with his vision for a brighter future. The residents of the capital city noticed almost immediately that the streets and hotel bars were no longer filled with drunken soldiers. Washingtonians marveled at the sight of fifty thousand men at a time marching flawlessly in straight columns with heads held high. By the sheer force of his personality, McClellan appeared to be turning the tide of the Civil War.

Of course, none of this was surprising to anyone who knew "the man on horseback's" pedigree. The son of a prestigious Philadelphia physician and a prominent socialite, McClellan had received the best education available. He had not only attended the most competitive schools, but had excelled there. He graduated second in his class at West Point and was already developing a distinguished record of service in the U.S. military. At only age 34, McClellan's potential for greatness seemed unlimited. Shortly after he assumed command, the young hero wrote to his wife "by some strange operation of magic [I have] become *the* power of the land….if the people call upon me to save the country—I *must* save it and cannot respect anything that is in the way." Now, in the early days of April 1862, destiny called General George McClellan to take his rightful place in history.

What happened next seemed a foregone conclusion.

Shortly after arriving at Fort Monroe, McClellan channeled his talent and tenacity into the charge of his impressive Army to Yorktown where he crushed the vastly outnumbered force of Confederate general Joe Johnston. With the much smaller Confederate force on its heels, McClellan continued marching his army fifty more miles to the Confederate capital of Richmond, Virginia. With no time to secure reinforcements, the Confederate

Army had no choice but to surrender their center of power—ending the American Civil War in June of 1862.

Or at least that's what *should* have happened. Sadly, it did not.

Instead what unfolded was a grim, cautionary tale that is every bit as relevant to 21st Century professionals as it was to Civil War commanders and 19th Century politicians.

When he arrived at Fort Monroe, McClellan immediately began doing what he did best—preparing. He strategized. He analyzed the enemy. He built roads. He fortified canons. He constructed bridges. He did everything *except* attack. On April 6, the famously patient Abraham Lincoln sent McClellan a telegram asking—in fact *begging*—him to act. "You now have over one hundred thousand troops…I think you better break the enemies' line from York-town to Warwick River at once. They will probably use *time* as advantageously as you can." Two more days passed and still nothing happened. On April 9, Lincoln sent another message. "It is indispensable to you that you strike a blow." With his characteristic empathy, Lincoln went on to write "The country will not fail to note—is now noting—that the present hesitation to move upon an intrenched (sic) enemy is but the story of Manassas repeated. I beg to assure you that I have never written you, or spoken to you, in greater kindness of feeling than now…*But you must act*."

Earlier that same year, after six months of delay from McClellan, Lincoln issued the formal General War Order No. 1. In it, he set February 22 as the day when the Union Army and Navy would begin its all-out offensive. February 22 came and went. Not until March 8 did McClellan finally begin moving his troops toward the significantly overmatched Confederate battalion camped in the town of Manassas. When he finally arrived, the promising young general discovered that the Confederates had already packed up their entire camp and moved on—averting what would have been a crushing defeat for them and an easy victory for McClellan. Most humiliating to McClellan, Lincoln and the entire populous of the northern states was the revelation that the Confederate "canons"— the same canons McClellan had argued were preventing him from attacking for the many months before then—turned out to be nothing more than wooden logs painted black.

Now, Lincoln feared that the same thing that happened in Manassas was happening all over again in Yorktown. A few weeks later, Lincoln's fears were confirmed. When McClellan's army arrived in Yorktown, Joe Johnston's Confederate army was gone. Worst of all, McClellan's indecision had given the strategically brilliant General Robert E. Lee time to bring substantial reinforcements to Johnston's aide.

Despite a personal visit from Lincoln in early May, McClellan simply could not bring himself to quit preparing and take action. By late June, General Lee had taken the fight to McClellan with one surprise offensive and a deadly series of attacks known as the Seven Days Battles. Well trained as they were, McClellan's soldiers fought skillfully and valiantly. Yet, since Lee consistently took the initiative to attack, he was able to decide the terms for which each battle was fought. Lee's decisive action caused McClellan to conclude in a telegraph to Lincoln's Secretary of War, Edward Stanton, that he was facing "vastly superior odds." He estimated that Lee was in command of no less than 200,000 men. In fact,

Lee had less than 100,000—far fewer than McClellan's force. Ultimately, McClellan concluded to Stanton and Lincoln that "I have lost this battle because my force was too small. I again repeat that I am not responsible for this." A few days later, McClellan retreated. It would take another three full years and hundreds of thousands of dead soldiers before either army would once again be in a position to end what remains the bloodiest battle in American history. By attempting to prevent his soldiers from getting in harm's way, McClellan ended up sending exponentially more soldiers to early graves over the next three years.

Through the contrasting lenses of McClellan's great failure on the battlefield and fast forwarding a century and a half to the Roundtable's big success in the corporate world, we can get a clear picture of what the decision process looks like from start to finish. To refresh your memory, each part of the Know-Think-Do framework maps to a simple 3-part process for habitually making strategically sound decisions more quickly and easily.

1. *Know.* Check Your Pulse.

2. *Think.* Consult An Anti-You.

3. *Do.* Be a Decider.

1. Check Your Pulse.

A clear Decision Pulse helps enhance both the speed and alignment of decision making by simplifying the process. We need to take a timeout here to clarify what I mean by "simple." Simplicity is a loaded word because it can come in two forms—ignorant simplicity and enlightened simplicity. Former U.S. Supreme Court Justice and a Civil War veteran himself, Oliver Wendell Holmes, once said "I would not give a fig for the simplicity on this side of complexity, but I would give my life for the simplicity on the other side of complexity." In other words, if we spend no time digging into the inherent complexity of a decision, the quality of that decision will likely suffer. We call that approach "ignorant simplicity" because it completely ignores the complex reality of the situation.

But clarifying a Decision Pulse enables you to wade through the complexity of your surrounding environment once to reveal a guiding principle for an entire category of future decisions. Since the Decision Pulse accounts for the environmental complexities surrounding your team or organization, remembering to "Check your Pulse," ensures your team members have paid adequate tribute to that complexity every time they make a decision. The complexity is baked into the Decision Pulse. Yet, at the same time, the team does not have to continue reinventing the wheel with every new decision. That's how the Decision Pulse breaks the tradeoff between speed and quality when making decisions.

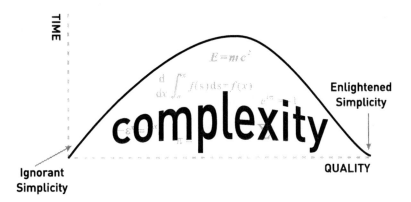

Remember the group of innovator's called the Roundtable at the health insurance conglomerate from chapter one? This group was stuck not because they couldn't come up with any good ideas, but because they couldn't decide which of the 37 great ideas to pursue. As part of our Decision Day workshop (or "D-Day") with the Roundtable, the team walked through Team Pulse discovery process. It turned out that what made this team uniquely valuable was their ability to "develop creative ideas unencumbered by bureaucracy." They used that Team Pulse to quickly narrow down the field of 37 options to less than five in a matter of minutes.

You could argue that McClellan and the Union Army also had a Decision Pulse. It was clear to virtually everyone who paid attention that the greatest weapon the Union Army had was size. Under Robert E. Lee's direction, few experts on either side of the Mason-Dixie line would have denied that the Confederate army had the best supreme commander available to American fighting forces during that era. Indeed Lincoln's first choice to command the Union Army was Lee. But as a native southerner, Lee felt he had to support the Confederacy. Given that fact, the Union Army's Decision Pulse would have been something along the lines of "THE bigger fighting force." McClellan seemed to embrace this idea by initially focusing on training this huge number of soldiers to fall in line as one impressively large, cohesive unit rather than practicing renegade tactics of the kind used by the militias in the American Revolutionary War. We know that the Union Army's leadership team of Lincoln, McClellan, and Edward Stanton paid attention to the size of each fighting force since it was frequently mentioned in their communications before each battle. So, it is possible that McClellan did check this Pulse before making his decisions to engage or not engage in battle. Step one is not where McClellan faltered.

2. Consult an Anti-You.

We already learned how the young leaders in the Roundtable consulted an Anti-You by running their ideas by their executive sponsors. McClellan also received plenty of Anti-You consultation in the form of letters from Stanton and personal visits from Lincoln. The key difference here is in the level of openness with which the decision makers received the advice. The Roundtable's general attitude was one of gratitude to the Anti-You's for taking the time to offer helpful advice. McClellan, on the other hand, was not so grateful for other points of view. In fact, McClellan despised them. He felt there was nothing about leading an Army that Lincoln or anyone else could tell him that he didn't already know. Here is where the first major problem arises with McClellan's decision process. In much the same way as I refused to consult an Anti-You before buying my RV, McClellan never sought the advice of his Anti-You's either. Step two in the decision process is something that the decision-maker must take responsibility for. It doesn't say "wait for your Anti-You to freely offer unsolicited advice." It says to "consult an Anti-You" because it is your responsibility to actively seek out the advice. Taking it upon yourself to consult an Anti-You not only increases your odds of arriving at a rational conclusion, it also has an important humbling effect. The act of asking for advice forces you to recognize that you might not have all the answers already. That's why it didn't matter that Lincoln and Stanton offered their advice. Since McClellan didn't go out of his way to seek it, he felt no obligation either to humble himself or to consider the merits of their suggestions to engage in battle sooner rather than later.

3. Be a Decider

Lastly, the decision-maker has no choice but to take decisive action. Once we had gone through the first two steps with the Roundtable, the only thing left to do was make a decision. In the course of a single day, the Roundtable decided to pursue an idea that eventually led to an innovative billing facilitation tool that would allow customers to easily access and view all of their insurance claims in a single place, rather than sifting through a maze of past hospital bills, clinic receipts, and credit card statements. In a period of four months, the team researched, compiled, and pitched the idea to the company's Innovation Council. One executive loved the idea and decided she wanted to start funding and developing the product right away. Was the billing tool The Roundtable's best idea? Maybe there was another idea that would have been even better? It's hard to say. The fact is that we will never know. What we do know is that they idea that they brought to life was a pretty darn good one. Additional months of calculation, speculation, and guesswork might have revealed a better idea and it might not have. That extra time spent hand-wringing would also sucked the enthusiasm out of the group and likely buried the institutional support they had in the beginning.

Instead of spending more time working to make a decision, the Roundtable focused on making their decision work.

Step three is where McClellan truly fell apart. Despite his immense talents, McClellan proved completely unable to quit preparing, and take decisive action. He always had a laundry list of excuses at the ready to explain why he simply could not take action until a later date. Sometimes he argued that the time was not right strategically—the battlefield was set up wrong, his force was too small, the timing wasn't right, and so on. Other times he hid behind a veil of righteous indignation about exposing his men to unnecessary danger. Like an overprotective parent, he argued it was his job to keep his men out of harm's way. A noble sentiment, but ultimately one that didn't square with the facts of the situation and ended up costing exponentially more lives in the long run. McClellan's favorite excuse for inaction was Lincoln. He claimed that Lincoln failed to provide him with enough men and supplies even though in reality he had twice as much of both relative to his opponents. We can spot the real reason McClellan delayed in his written explanation for his first battle and his first loss: "I have lost this battle because my force was too small. I again repeat that I am not responsible for this." His forceful, almost childish, denial of responsibility for the battle's outcome tips McClellan's hand. More than anything, McClellan was afraid of being responsible for failing. If I'm honest that is probably the number one reason why I behave indecisively sometime. And maybe that rings true for you as well? Unless the Confederate army all but laid down their guns at his feet, McClellan wasn't going to take the chance of acting.

At the end of the day, this fear of failing, being wrong, or making a mistake, more than any other cause is responsible for inaction. As long as we continue to prepare, and to gather data, and to strategize, it is impossible for us to definitively lose. Just like those fine betting establishments, state lotteries, like to remind people "you can't win if you don't play" we also like to subtly remind ourselves that the reverse is true. We often act as though we can't *lose* if we don't play. While it is true that you can't be rejected if you don't make the call, or ask for the date. And you can't lose a game if you never play. But as McClellan (and Neville Chamberlain, for that matter) found out, sooner or later you can absolutely lose the war as well as many of your soldiers and citizens by endlessly delaying action.

The same is true with making a decision and taking decisive action. Especially, if you are in a leadership position, sooner or later you won't be able to outrun a decision. Circumstances will eventually bring the decision to your doorstep in a way that might not be as favorable as it once was.

At another level, this step is also where Lincoln stumbled, as he would later admit. Lincoln was afraid to replace McClellan because he initially showed so much promise and talent in virtually all other areas of military command, and because he had been so popular. Lincoln was afraid to quit on McClellan until it was too late and any advantage his Army had was all but lost. By the time he replaced McClellan, Lee's armies had fully regrouped and were as strong as ever. Logically speaking, he likely knew that McClellan was wrong for the job months before he actually quit on him. Weeks before the false start at Yorktown, Lincoln tried to persuade McClellan to take action by suggesting that the Confederate generals "will probably use *time* as advantageously as you can." In one of those ironic twists befitting of a Greek tragedy, Lincoln found out that his wisdom applied as much to himself as it did to McClellan.

EXECUTIVE SUMMARY

- Indecision made the American Civil War three times longer and deadlier than it could have been.

- A simple, effective decision process consists of three steps:

    1. Checking your pulse.

    2. Consulting your anti-you.

    3. Being a decider.

- "I would not give a fig for the simplicity on this side of complexity, but I would give my life for the simplicity on the other side of complexity." –Oliver Wendell Holmes

- Defining a Team Decision Pulse enabled the Roundtable to successfully move from ignorant simplicity to enlightened simplicity.

- Consulting an anti-you requires the humility that comes with seeking advice. The Roundtable expressed the humility that George McClellan never could.

- The Roundtable chose to spend less time working to make their decisions, and more time making their decisions work.

- One of Lincoln's greatest mistakes was his failure to heed his own advice that the enemy "will probably use *time* as advantageously as you can."

CHAPTER EIGHT

PERSONALITY: DEFINING DECISION STYLES

"Knowing yourself is the beginning of wisdom."

--Aristotle

The Know, Think, Do process is a roadmap. It tells us where strategic direction, logical reasoning techniques, and decisive action are located in relation to one another in your pursuit of excellence. But in order for a map to be useful you have to know where you are starting from. For example, even if I know that Chicago is my desired destination, my trip is going to look very different if my drive starts in New York versus Los Angeles. Your personal Decision Style indicates your starting point for using the 3-step strategic behavior process.

Some people will *know* the strategic direction very well at the conceptual level, enabling them to see the big picture quite clearly. Others will *know* how it works at a more operational level, allowing them to see what tactics will support it. Some people will *think* about the strategy and the corresponding options from a more cautious perspective, while others will analyze it from a more risk-tolerant angle. Some people will lean towards *doing* sooner or later depending on whether they tend to be more impulsive or more deliberative. Combining those three preferences gives you your Decision Style. No preference is generally better or worse than another. Each style has its own strengths and weaknesses, and a weakness in one situation could be a strength in another situation.

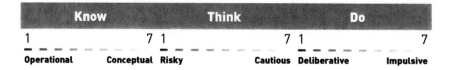

Identifying your Decision Style offers two key benefits. First, it enables you to define the boundaries of your comfort zone, and gives you an idea of where to find your blind spots. The second reason is that it helps you get a feel for how the individuals in your team approach decisions individually, which sheds light on how they may decide as a group.

1. Know: Conceptual vs. Operational

Truly successful strategic behavior requires understanding the strategy at both the 30,000 feet conceptual level and at the ground level where day-to-day operations happen. People that tend to be more conceptual enjoy spotting trends and playing with ideas. When they think of the strategic direction, they tend to think about what it means in the bigger picture of the company's competitive landscape and what opportunities and threats could be waiting for them on the horizon. When discussions start dropping down into the weeds, people with a conceptual preference tend to lose energy. On the other hand, if you're always looking at the horizon, immediate threats and opportunities can go unnoticed. It is easy to step right over the $100 bill laying on the sidewalk, or to trip on the wrinkle in the carpet. Too much conceptual thinking can also lead to brilliant theories that have zero impact on real-world results. You don't want to make yourself the butt of the old joke about economists where one says to the other "Sure, it might work in practice. But does it work in theory?"

People with an operational bent are very tactical in their orientation to strategy. They enjoy immersing themselves in operational details and prefer to focus their energy on translating strategic priorities into actionable steps. Defining the overall direction or broader vision is less important to them than defining how to execute that vision with maximum efficiency. The challenge for operational people is to avoid falling victim to Peter Drucker's warning that "there is nothing quite so useless as doing efficiently that which should not be done at all."

As with all of the preferences, almost nobody is *all* conceptual or *all* operational *all* of the time. The conceptual and operational labels are just opposite ends of a spectrum. For example, the Decision Styles Index™ measures people on a scale of zero to seven where zero is extremely operational and seven is extremely conceptual. My preference is very conceptual. That is most likely why writing and researching books energizes me instead of sucking the life out of me. However, I'm also the CEO of a business, so I've forced myself to learn how to be more operational when the situation calls for it. Yet, I still know that operations are not my strength. That's why the first person I added to my payroll was a Chief Operating Officer. When it comes to making decisions I lean on my COO to think of the operational implications of our strategic direction.

2. Think: Risky vs. Cautious

Some people are more comfortable taking risks where others tend to be more cautious. The biggest difference tends to be in which elements of the situation people focus on. People that we commonly regard as "risk-takers" don't actually prefer to take risks if they can help it. They like a no-risk slam dunk just as much as the next guy. The difference is that they simply focus more on the potential reward than the possible downside. For example, the riskier person might be more comfortable pursuing two birds in the bush, whereas the cautious person contents himself with the one bird in hand. The possibility of the double reward is enough to convince them to incur the risk. However, even the so-called risk-taker won't usually let go of the bird in the hand just to pursue *one* bird in the bush. That's not brave. That's just dumb.

These preferences will often affect the way you think about your options when making strategic decisions. For example, let's say your team has decided that your Decision Pulse is to be "THE innovation authority" in your industry. Everyone on the team fully believes in that direction. However, risk preferences might lead you to different approaches. Riskier team members might push for obtaining the "first mover advantage." I've found that approximately 75% of riskier people prefer to be "the first to try something new."

In comparison, cautious people are three times more likely to consider risks before making a decision. That means more cautious team members might support a calculated delay before releasing a new product. The rule of thumb at Apple Computer in the 1980s was to create a new technology, and even "leak" their technological advance to a few startups before releasing the product. This way the startup bore the greatest risks of building consumer interest in an untested market. Then by the time Apple came out with its version of the product, a solid market for it already existed. With Apple's much stronger distribution channels, they could focus on significantly growing the market that the startup had built and also introduce a far superior rendition of the product they knew people already wanted. Of course that approach also presented a risk of the startup getting too far ahead, and establishing themselves as the clear leader. But that risk felt much smaller than the risk of releasing a product that nobody wanted. Similarly, in the 1990s when Target stores were etching out their competitive position in a discount retail world dominated by Wal-Mart, their IT department decided that they would support the company's growth by always being the *second* adopter of new technologies. They believed that embracing new technologies could give them a competitive edge. However, they also knew that first edition technologies were almost always riddled with glitches that the manufacturer wouldn't fix until version 2.0 hit the market.

The exact risk recipe will be different for every team and every organization. We found no strong evidence that one preference actually produces better outcomes than another. Sometimes risks pay off, and sometimes they don't. What is important for you to know is which way you lean, and the basic risk makeup of your team. In the general population we find that about three out of four people tend to fall on the cautious side of the equation, whereas one in four tend to be riskier. But that will vary depending on the exact group. That ratio of risky to cautious people was exactly the opposite for our clients within a newly created mobile phone division of a multi-national electronics retailer. The parent company was much closer to the normal 3:1 cautious to risky ratio. But the self-proclaimed "cowboys" who wanted to ride out to this new frontier for the company tended to be much more comfortable exposing themselves to risk for the possibility of a higher reward. The conservative composition of the people at headquarters was probably valuable for sustaining the large company's health, whereas the bolder decision-makers were necessary for launching the new division.

3. Do: Deliberative vs. Impulsive

Finally, some people like to think less about a decision before jumping into action, while others prefer thinking more. The distinction between these two preferences has two important implications. The first is time. Our research showed that people with an impulsive preference were five times more likely to report that they make their best decisions while under time pressure. In contrast, 72% of deliberative people said they make their worst decisions under time pressure. Of course this was all self-reported data so we can't know precisely how good their decisions really were in either case. But the widely differing perceptions speak volumes about how these people approach the act of making a decision. Impulsive people put a premium on the speed of action and tend to be more comfortable figuring things out as they go rather than taking a "wait-and-see" approach. That isn't just because they think it saves time; it is because they actually believe they make better decisions in those situations. That penchant for action can be a tremendous asset to personal and team success in the right environment. However, decision quality can also suffer if the bias for action becomes an excuse for impatience or lazy thinking.

For deliberative people, intellectual problems are often an adventure as much as they are an obstacle. Not only do they believe more thought will lead to better decisions, they simply enjoy the act of digging into complex problems as much as they enjoy arriving at a decision. Thinking for the sake of thinking can be fun for deliberative people, and so they are comfortable withholding judgment until they've had a chance to dig deep and play around in the complexity of a situation. When that preference is taken to extremes, the deliberator can sometimes become paralyzed by analysis and hinder progress.

The second, less obvious implication relates to how these tendencies affect team decisions. President Harry Truman once said he desperately wanted to find a one-armed advisor, because all he ever heard from his Washington advisors was "on the other hand..." Truman was likely surrounded by very bright people with a deliberative preference who loved diving into complex problems. This stood in stark contrast to his own impulsive leanings and strong bias toward action. Many impulsive people share Truman's outlook. This probably explains why impulsive people report that the one thing that makes them most uncomfortable when making decisions is the involvement of other people. Put another way, impulsive people tend to spend much less effort on building consensus before taking action. Part of the reason that deliberative people prefer to spend more time reaching a decision is that they give themselves enough time to collect everyone's input and to build agreement going forward.

Building consensus can be valuable. Decisions need to have buy-in if they are going to be properly executed, and many people resent being excluded from the decision process when the decision directly impacts them. On the other hand (apologies to President Truman), consensus is not always possible or desirable. Consensus is all too often used by managers as an excuse to avoid making difficult decisions. For example, in 1854 the U.S. Senator Stephen Douglas passed the Kansas-Nebraska Act in an attempt to keep the peace between the North and the South on the increasingly divisive issue of slavery. Ostensibly, the Act was a triumph for democracy because it allowed citizens in the new states of Kansas and Nebraska to decide for themselves whether slavery would be legal in their states. Conveniently for Douglas, this also prevented him and his allies from having to make a public decision about whether or not they supported slavery. The result for Kansas and Nebraska was a massive influx of people on both sides of the slavery debate, which led to a bloody conflict foreshadowing the Civil War that began just seven years later.

The truth is that sometimes we have to make win-lose decisions in which some people will not get their way. With deference to

Jim Collins, sometimes the Tyranny of the Or is not the problem. It is actually the Tyranny of the And that creates the obstacle to greatness. Some issues simply have little room for compromise or consensus and they require us to quit pleasing some group of stakeholders in order to move forward for the long term good of the most stakeholders. Make no mistake, this can be painful, but it is sometimes necessary. On the other hand, the best leaders do not use this simple truth as an excuse for steamrolling their teams. Their approach gives everyone a voice. However, they make it clear that the final decision will be the one that is best for the team, not the one that tries to make everyone happy.

4. Using Decision Styles to Make Team Decisions

As a general rule, the best team decisions result from diversity and debate. Good team decisions require a blend of opposing Decision Styles, and questions that uncover multiple perspectives. To aid the debate, I recommend using a few specific questions for each phase of the decision process.

During the Know phase, you should focus on answering these questions:

- What is our Decision Pulse?

- Which of these options will enable our team to most effectively advance the top strategic priority?

During the Think phase, you should focus on answering these questions:

- Do any of these options present unnecessary risks that can be avoided?

- How could we creatively minimize the risk for the big bet, high-reward option?

- What is the cost of passing up the higher-reward option?

During the Do phase, you should focus on answering these questions:

- Are we missing essential information that could be obtained with very little effort?

- What is the cost of delaying the decision?

- Have we reached the point where there is nothing left to do but quit on some of the options?

Ultimately, it is the team leader's job to ensure that the team makes a decision. That decision will rarely fully satisfy everyone in the group, and you should resist the urge to try to keep everyone happy. All too often attempts to please everyone end up pleasing no one. Sometimes, the only way to move forward is by actively quitting on one stakeholder's (or group of stakeholder's) concerns. You should acknowledge their concerns and show them respect, and then make the right decision. It's an unfortunate truth. But by helping your team identify their decision styles and to better understand the process you are going through to make the decision, even those who didn't get their way will be much more likely to respect the decision and productively execute it.

EXECUTIVE SUMMARY

- The 3-part decision process is like a map. Your Decision Style is like the GPS for your map.

- Some people will prefer to Know the strategy at conceptual level, while others will approach it at a more operational level.

- Some people will Think about decisions more cautiously, while others tend to be more tolerant of risk.

- Some people prefer to deliberate more before they Do things, while others tend to jump in more impulsively.

- For team decisions collaboration is good, but consensus can be dangerous.

CHAPTER NINE

PRESSURE: A FORCE FOR GOOD

"Everybody's got a plan
until they get punched in the mouth."

--Mike Tyson

In 2006, the U.S. Forest Service (Smokey Bear's employer) issued a report. The Chief of the Forest Service, Dale Bosworth stated that one of the greatest threats facing America's national forests is the accumulation of unburned fuel ladders that could ignite to create a tragically dangerous and destructive fire. Since forest fires had not been allowed to burn on federal lands since 1988, seven out of every 10 U.S. forests were in grave danger of a catastrophic wildfire that could not be controlled. Now, here is the really unsettling thing: Given that knowledge from their own report, guess what percent of fires the Forest Service allowed to burn that very year the report came out? One. One measly percent.

Despite all that they knew about fire's restorative value for the forests they exist to protect, the U.S. Forest Service has been unable to bring itself to *quit* fighting fires.

The question is *why*? The answer is *pressure*.

1. The Dark Side of Pressure

The U.S. Forest Service has both push pressures and pull pressures moving them away from strategic behavior. On the one hand, the people in the communities surrounding the federal lands are *pushing* the Forest Service to squash every fire immediately. They do not want their local habitat decimated or their homes, businesses, and other properties burned. Understandably so. But years of suppressing every fire possible has created a situation in which the forests have become their own worst enemy. Calling to mind a few other sectors of Americana, the forest have been implicitly deemed "too big to fail."

The Forest Service is also being *pulled* in the same direction by an enticing incentive. In the year following the Yellowstone Fires, Congress tripled the U.S. Forest Service's annual budget for suppressing fires. But since the Forest Service had an "absolute suppression" policy in place since 1908, even this dramatically expanded budget barely put a dent in their huge deficit. Putting out every fire that sparks in every national forest every single year is a somewhat costly endeavor. Today, the Forest Service receives an annual budget for putting out fires. It's a line item on their overall budget just like pens and staplers. But in a nifty arrangement set up in 1993 with the Federal Treasury, if one or more Acts of God create so much fire in one year that the Forest Service has to spend over their budgeted amount, then Uncle Sam allows them to pull from an emergency fund. Apparently, God has been very active since 1993. The only logical conclusion is that Kurt Cobain's passing shortly after that so disturbed God that he reigned down enough fire to force the Forest Service to pull from the emergency fund every single year since the emergency fund was created.

But before we rush out to chastise the leadership of the U.S. Forest Service, we should put ourselves in their shoes: If you were running the U.S. Forest Service and you were responsible for the jobs of thousands of men and women, and you had to personally answer to angry citizens and powerful politicians who either don't understand or don't care about the ecology of forests, and you had what is effectively an unlimited budget that only grew bigger the more fires you suppressed, would you quit fighting fires? Honestly?

The truth is that even if you arm yourself with the right strategic decision Process, and construct a team with just the right blend of Personality traits, systemic Pressure can thwart your best efforts at strategic behavior.

The good news is that pressure, much like fire, can also be used for good.

2. The Bright Side of Pressure

In 1999, proud parent Hewlett Packard gave birth to Agilent Technologies. The first two years after it left the nest, the sky appeared to be the limit for the fledgling maker of semiconductors and other technology components. Then in 2001 those lofty aspirations tumbled to the ground when the stock market bubble burst. Within just three quarters, Agilent's revenues fell nearly

60%. For Agilent and many others the stock market crash in 2001 was like the lightning that struck the lodgepole pine trees in Yellowstone. As you might expect, this caused a significant belt-tightening that touched every corner of the business. Emergency efforts to stay afloat included tactics ranging from the layoff of 8,000 employees to the shrinking of that year's all black and white, *sans* graphics annual report to shareholders.

But the calamity also did something else. Agilent's Vice President of Global Talent at the time, Kirk Froggatt, said that almost overnight company managers had to "stop touching many things, but mastering nothing." Some otherwise talented managers who couldn't make the tough decisions fast enough, eventually found themselves repurposed. In addition to Froggat, Agilent's 2001 brush with bankruptcy also made a powerful and lasting impact on a manager named William "Bill" Sullivan.

Bill Sullivan had spent the majority of his career with Hewlett Packard. When Agilent spun off from its parent company, Sullivan went along as Agilent's Chief Operating Officer. Sullivan had always advocated for focus, often reciting his mentor David Packard's famous quote that "more companies die from overeating than starvation." Following 2001, however, Sullivan developed what must have seemed like an almost obsessive appreciation for decisiveness. "That's the basis of being a manager—you gotta make a decision," Sullivan recently told an audience of MBA students at his alma mater. Four years later when Sullivan was awarded the top job at Agilent, he immediately began putting his preaching into practice. In an abrupt about-face reminiscent of Steve Jobs circa 1997, Sullivan divested everything outside of Agilent's scientific testing and measurement business. While this was an important strategic move for the company, it was not especially novel. Ever since Bruce Henderson built his Boston Consulting Group on advising clients to cut loose their dogs in favor of their cash cows and stars, moves like this have been a part of nearly all CEO's strategic playbooks. What made Sullivan's move somewhat unique, however, is that he sold off Agilent's entire semiconductor business—the very business in which he had grown up. That would have been something like Howard Schultz proclaiming that Starbucks was going to sell off its coffee business and focus only on breakfast sandwiches. But even that was not Sullivan's greatest contribution to our knowledge of strategic behavior and leadership.

Sullivan's true genius was in recognizing that ultimate success or failure of his strategy would have less to do with the decisions *he* made, than the collective quality of decisions made by his managers throughout the organization. The brush with bankruptcy in 2001 had taught him that it wasn't only the C-level leaders who needed to be decisive. Decisiveness had to be baked into the culture so that managers at every level knew how to consistently make tough decisions with speed and clarity. So in addition to his constant reminders that "it's the second decision that matters," in 2006 Sullivan enlisted Kirk Froggat to help institutionalize his belief. Froggat and his team created what they called the "Speed to Opportunity Index." The Speed to Opportunity index consisted of a few basic questions they asked employees to answer about their boss's speed and decisiveness. According to Sullivan "when eight out of 10 your employees say you can't make a decision, that's a problem." But managers are imperfect human beings so they have lots of problems and not all of them get addressed by the organization. The Speed to Opportunity Index highlighted a certain set of behaviors that ensured this particular problem was one that the company addressed in prompt fashion. Within three years of introducing the new metric, Agilent's managers jumped from the 50th percentile to the 82nd percentile in speed/decisiveness relative to managers in other companies and in similar industries. Today, Bill Sullivan says the first question we ask our employees about their manager is "can they make a decision?"

When Kevin Wilde and I initially spoke about his research we were both pretty excited by his findings. He had tapped into something with profound implications for personal and professional success. But as a learning and development specialist, the question Wilde really wanted answered was whether these skills can be learned, or whether they are fixed abilities? It was a question I wanted answered as well.

When I interviewed Tim Judge about his research on core self-evaluations for a 2009 article I wrote in my column for *Bloomberg Business Week*, I posed a similar question to him. Given that it was such a considerable success factor, I wanted to know whether or not the organization could somehow implant a higher core self-evaluation into their individual workers? After all, that is one of the promises of the positive psychology movement within organizations: you can do it! Unfortunately, Judge did not affirm my hopes. "I am somewhat dubious about changing people's CSE," Judge told me. "We have another study in progress (of identical twins reared apart) where we found that CSE was substantially inherited. Moreover, interventions designed to raise CSE are fraught with problems and, as with many interventions, they cease to be effective once the intervention is over."

Yet at Agilent not only did a single manager improve on speed and decisiveness, an entire population of managers made a substantial improvement. How do we explain the contradiction?

The explanation is this: The core self-evaluation is a belief. Decisiveness is a behavior. The question I asked Tim Judge was different than the one we are asking here. Although the research shows that having a high core self-evaluation will likely provide you with a head start on decisiveness, the two concepts are not exactly the same. It is difficult to call anything a "law" in the social sciences, but one thing we can say with a high degree of certainty is that behaviors can be changed, even if underlying mental states and beliefs remain steady. Tim Judge is most likely correct in his assertion that even if you can change the core belief temporarily, it will probably slip back to its baseline level once the change effort is over. But the belief is not our primary concern. The resulting behavior is all we are really interested in. The beauty of Agilent's approach is that the "intervention"—the measurement—is built right into their regular performance evaluations. As long as their managers continue receiving performance evaluations on their speed to opportunity, the "intervention" will continue.

Agilent's introduction of the Speed to Opportunity index is a terrific example of a push pressure. The metric pushes people out of the nest and continues nudging them to be more decisive even if they aren't totally comfortable doing so. It stretches them. Despite the flurry of recent interest in the power of intrinsic motivation, the old maxim that "you get what you measure" still holds true here. Of course the caveat is that simply ordering people to "be more decisive or you're fired" is probably a recipe for disaster. If they don't understand the company's strategic direction or how that strategy applies to their particular team's activities (i.e. if they don't know what their Team Decision Pulse is) then the pressure will create more impulsiveness than it will decisiveness. That is why this kind of pressure must be coupled with a clear understanding of the full decision process.

According to Froggat, Sullivan had spent years informally coaching his teams and direct reports on the proper way to take focused, decisive action. He provided no more than one or two top strategic objectives for the company each year. I n other words, he had already sown the seeds of a decisive culture before the formal Speed to Opportunity measure was introduced. There is a reason why this chapter on Pressure comes after the chapter on Process. If you try to leapfrog the Process and Personality pieces, and suddenly spring a speed and decisiveness metric on your managers, you will more than likely end up with nothing but rash behaviors that make little strategic sense. After you educate your managers on the Know-Think-Do framework, you can add a few additional questions focused on speed and decisiveness to your existing 360 feedback survey or your chosen performance feedback tool.

This approach is not only an incredibly simple way of reinforcing the learning and practice of the framework on an ongoing basis, it also has the advantage of shaping the culture. The simple act of asking employees to answer the questions about their managers sends a clear message that "speed and decisiveness matter here."

The importance of the latter message cannot be overstated. When I deliver speeches I often share my favorite Dilbert cartoon. In the strip, Dilbert's boss tells Dilbert "My job is to encourage people to take risks...my other job is to punish people who make any kind of mistake. My point is that I'm glad I don't have your job." All too often we see the top leadership in an organization singing the praises of risk-taking and the value of "failing fast" as a learning tool. Yet down in the trenches, everyone knows the real truth. You get an irreversible black mark on your record for risks that don't pan out. Sometimes that black mark leads to a pink slip. As one Fortune 100 executive told me, "the risks for my career of taking a risk for the company far outweigh any financial gain I could create."

Kevin Wilde is all too aware of this phenomenon. After discovering the general performance impact of taking bold, decisive action, one of the first things he looked at was what happened to the managers at General Mills who demonstrated these behaviors. Fortunately, he discovered that General Mills was already systematically supporting these behaviors. Managers who showed up as high on both strategic judgment and boldness, were also twice as likely to be found in that elite group of employees who were rated as both high potential and high performing. "The message was clear," Wilde said. "At General Mills, we reward for this."

EXECUTIVE SUMMARY

- Systemic pressure is like fire—it can hinder growth or it can help it.

- The U.S. Forest Service was pushed by the community stakeholders and pulled by federal incentives to keep suppressing forest fires despite the long term dangers.

- Agilent Technologies used the pressure of performance measurement to encourage decisive quitting. Kirk Frogatt's implementation of the Speed to Opportunity index generated a 32% improvement in speed and decisiveness company-wide in just three years.

- Like all behaviors, decisiveness is sensitive to external punishments and incentives. Organizations can implement simple measurement tools that provide just the right amount of pressure to create decisive cultures.

CONCLUSION

LIVE STRATEGICALLY

"The crucial thing is to find the truth which is true for me. To find the idea for which I am to live and die...So that I could base the development of my thoughts not on something called 'objective'—something which is not my own—but upon something which is bound up with the deepest roots of my existence. To which I cling fast even though the whole world may collapse. This is what I need and this is what I strive for."

–Soren Kierkegaard

As you read in the beginning, this book was written to help you develop the skills you need to pursue excellence strategically all day, every day. That means at home as well as at work. Your decisions are the "deliverables" of strategic behavior. But knowledge and skills only tell part of the story of strategic behavior. You also have to be motivated. A very simple formula for human performance of almost every kind is this:

SKILL x MOTIVATION = PERFORMANCE

In this case, Skill x Motivation = *Strategic* Performance. For example, you might have what it takes to be an excellent chess player. But if you really like to play basketball and hate playing chess, you won't be motivated to practice playing chess very often and your performance will eventually suffer. On the other hand, I might want to be the world's best basketball player, but I don't have much (read: *any*) talent for the sport. By practicing every day, I could get much better at playing. But without being tall or able to jump high, and possessing very average—and possibly downright *poor*—hand-eye coordination, no amount of motivation will land me a contract in the NBA. High performance requires both skill and motivation. The previous chapters have focused primarily on the skill part of the equation. We touched a little bit on motivation in the chapter on Pressure, but external pressure is only one kind of motivation—extrinsic motivation. Another kind is intrinsic motivation, which is much more personal.

In this final chapter, we are going to close on a personal note. The same strategic behavior principles you've read about all through the book apply to your pursuit of excellence in your life as well as in your work.

1. Know Your Personal Pulse

Imagine this: At the end of your company's fiscal year, the higher-ups announce they have decided to implement a new reward system. Eligible employees will be able to select an award from the following options. Eligibility is based on performance as determined by your manager, but ever since you read this amazing book about Strategic Behavior, your ridiculously high performance makes you more than eligible. So, you may choose one of the following options:

1. An $8,000 cash payment, less taxes and withholdings
2. A $6,0000 contribution to the company's Employee Stock Purchase Plan

3. An additional 3 weeks of paid time off (can be carried over if unused during the current year)

4. Airfare and 1 week's lodging at an African Safari

5. Participation in the week-long Executive Leadership Team's strategic planning offsite at the CEO's ski lodge in Vail, CO.

6. Airfare and 1 week's lodging for four anywhere in the continental U.S.

7. Airfare and 1 week's lodging to participate in Habitat for Humanity in Central America, Africa or Asia.

8. 1 week as Assistant Leader of your department with responsibility for recommending how work is allocated across your team.

Your choice likely reflects your Personal Pulse. Over the past few decades, researchers ranging from cultural psychologists like Shalom Schwartz at Hebrew University to organizational psychologists like Daniel Cable and Jeffrey Edwards at the University of North Carolina have determined that there are eight universal values shared by virtually every culture on earth from stock traders in the U.S. and farmers in South Africa to auto mechanics in China, visual artists in Brazil, movie stars, moms, dads, and middle managers. If you're like 99.99% of people on the planet, you'll agree that at least six and — and as many as eight — of these directions are important to you. They are:

- **Humanity.** Making the world a better place.

- **Relationships.** Developing deep, close bonds with family and friends.

- **Authority.** Having self-discipline and bringing pride to your family.

- **Security.** Keeping the people you care about safe, happy and healthy.

- **Power.** Gaining recognition and respect for your accomplishments.

- **Achievement.** Making progress on personal goals.

- **Stimulation.** Having fun and keeping life interesting.

- **Freedom.** Staying independent and open to opportunity.

(*See Appendix A for a deeper look at each of the eight personal directions.*)

Each direction is as valid and valuable as any other. None of them sound particularly unsatisfying. Of course, that is the problem. You know by now that eight directions is seven too many if you're trying to get somewhere. You can't let the smell of cheese from very profitable breakfast sandwiches overpower the smell of coffee if you are "THE coffee authority," and you have to deny the request of some customers who want an in-flight meal if it raises costs at "THE low-fare airline." Similarly, you will almost certainly have to let go of that desire for freedom and independence if you really want to move yourself in the direction of prestige and achievement by taking that promotion with all of its extra responsibility and 90-hour work weeks. On the other hand, it would be a bad idea to pass up the opportunity to take the promotion just because a friend tells you that he/she wouldn't want to give up his/her independence. *You* are not your friend and your friend is not you. Starbucks has a different strategic direction than Panera Bread. Southwest Airlines has a different direction than Delta Airlines. Strategic behavior in your personal life abides by the same principles as strategic behavior at a multi-national corporation—strategy is all about using your direction to decide what *not* to do.

The only way to make a strategic life decision is to know what the strategic direction or Personal Decision Pulse is for *your* life, and then consciously quit pursuing the options that get in the way of moving in that direction. A great place to start is with those eight universal values. You can take a short free online assessment to find your Personal Pulse by going to DecisionPulse.com. Much like we discussed in the chapter on strategic rationality, this direction is merely a hypothesis about what you care most about and it will likely require some testing and revising in real world situations. I learned a lot of about what exactly Freedom meant to me after buying that motorhome.

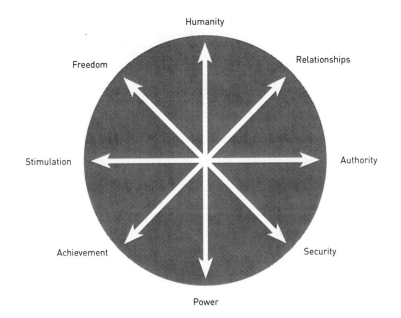

2. Pursuing a Life of Excellence

Many working people today ferociously pursue work-life balance. Since you can now fit an entire workstation into the pocket of your jeans, you can work from anywhere at any time. Balance has never been easier! (Thank you, smartphones!) However, as one executive coach explained to me after a talk I gave: "I tell my clients that if we hold work off to the side in one hand, and our lives off to the side in the other hand, it often feels more like crucifixion than balance." I'd like to suggest a slightly different approach than balance.

The few people who appear to have truly achieved work/life balance—you know, the people who do well at their jobs without sacrificing nights and weekends with their families, friends or hobbies—are not balanced at all. They have clearly chosen life over work. That does not mean that their careers are not important to them. They just have a clearer idea than most people about where work fits within the bigger picture of their life. That enables them to be strategic. They understand the strategic tradeoff they are making. Instituting a non-negotiable deadline for themselves in which they go home at 5 p.m. every night so they can have dinner with their families means that this could hurt their chances of advancing their career. But they know that, and they have already decided what their primary direction is. They will do whatever they can to advance their career *except* sacrifice important time with their families. It is just like how Southwest Airlines will do whatever they can to make their customers happy *except* sacrifice their position as THE low-fare airline.

At some level, everyone's work must be in service to their life. But work can serve many different strategic directions in many different people's lives. For some people, the strategic direction of their life requires them to be workaholics. Former General Electric CEO, Jack Welch was well known for being a workaholic and priding himself on working 80-hour weeks his entire career. But for Welch that was exactly what he wanted for his life. Nothing made him happier than "winning" as he titled his 2005 book. He admits with some tone of regret that his working style cost him a couple of marriages and a lot of time with his kids, but on the whole he wouldn't have changed it. Before we round up the posse to go tar and feather those greedy workaholics, we should remember that Mother Theresa was a workaholic, too. She worked every waking hour of every day serving the untouchables in Calcutta, India. She clearly chose the Humanity direction for herself. Jack Welch and Mother Theresa chose strategic directions that could not be more opposite, and yet both behaved very strategically, accepting enormous tradeoffs. Welch admits that his tradeoffs cost him two marriages. Mother Theresa willing sacrificed any chance of having even one marriage because of her tradeoff to become a nun and serve the Untouchables. Millions of other people consciously quit their pursuit for extraordinary career success specifically to protect their marriages or other personal interests. Whether it is your neighbor who routinely passes up promotions in order to avoid travel and protect her Relationships at home, or Jack Welch and Mother Theresa who sacrificed family lives for Achievement and Humanity, all of them generated strategic momentum for their lives.

The truth is that I have no idea whether you should become a workaholic or start working less. If there has ever been a question that is above one's pay grade, this question is way above mine. I can't tell you what the meaning of your life is, let alone what is the meaning of all life. I can tell you what psychologists know about "meaning" as a psychological construct. Meaning has two basic components to it. One component is about purpose. Purpose is about answering why are you here on earth? Many believe this has something to do with helping others and leaving some kind of a social legacy. Your answer to this question will likely have a lot to do with your spiritual beliefs, or lack of spiritual beliefs.

The second component is a bit more earthly. It has to do with making sense of how the various pieces in your life fit together. If purpose is more of a transcendental or spiritual question, then harmony is much more of a practical question. For example, if you are working 100-hour weeks at a corporate sponsor of genocide, but your personal direction is Humanity, you are probably not living a harmonious life. In fact, that dissonance will make it really difficult to generate sustainable strategic momentum in your life or your work. Similarly, if your strategic direction is Power and yet you find yourself working at a small, local charity with no office and limited resources, it will be just as hard to generate strategic momentum for your life no matter how much good your employer does for society. In both of these cases, your job and your life are not reinforcing each other.

Obviously, these are extreme examples. Your situation will likely fall somewhere in between. There is rarely a one-to-one relationship between a certain direction and a certain job. To an outsider, some jobs that seem clearly unfit for some personal directions might not be what they appear. For example, Adam Grant is a friend and colleague who is a professor at the Wharton School of Business and the author of *Give and Take*. Before Adam turned 30, he became the youngest professor to ever receive tenure at the prestigious business school well known for cranking out a steady supply of so-called "Masters of the Universe" who make their home at Wall Street investment banks. Yet, Adam's personal direction is Humanity. You might guess that there is a serious lack of harmony here. Actually, however, he has strategically aligned his job perfectly with his personal direction. He has established himself as one of the world's leading researchers on the ways in which meaningful work impacts individual and organizational financial performance. In particular, he has conducted a number of fascinating experiments revealing how leaders who go out of their way to show their people how their work benefits their fellow human beings, also reap incredible gains in productivity and performance for the organization. In other words, he has very convincingly and very quickly by the standards of academia, amassed an ironclad case—respected by academics and practitioners alike—for why humanitarians truly do build more successful businesses not in spite of their emphasis on humanity, but because of it.

The point is that changing the way in which you approach your job can often resolve what might at first seem to be a disconnect. So if you find your personal direction only to realize that your job is moving you in a different direction, try adapting your job to your direction before writing off your job altogether. In order to successfully adapt your job and its reward structure, you have to do two things. First, you have to know what your personal direction is. It is your responsibility to identify your direction and clarify what it means to you and how it could fit with your job. It is not your company's or your boss's responsibility to guess what makes your life meaningful and then try to reward you appropriately. If they don't know what your direction is, then it really is not their fault if they reward you incorrectly.

Secondly, you have to be good at your job. At a panel discussion of corporate learning leaders, Cindy Johnson, the head of learning and leadership development at innovation powerhouse 3M, was asked by an audience member how young people in the workforce could get more respect and autonomy in their organizations. Her pointed response was "do something really well." In other words, performing at a level barely above the mediocrity line will not inspire your manager or your company to bend over backwards accommodating your personal preferences. The fact is that people who are more valuable to their teams and their companies have more leverage when it comes to customizing their work and their rewards than do people who are less valuable. It might not be fair. But in my experience with a vast number of companies big and small, old and new this simply is the reality. People whom the manager does not want to lose will be granted more latitude and flexibility than people whose performance makes them more or less replaceable. Regardless of the official company policy or what the official stance on work-life balance is according to the promotional materials in Human Resources brochures, you will always have more bargaining power the better you are at your job. People do get treated differently. Even in a hard-driving performance culture where most people work incredibly long hours and rarely take vacations, high performers will be granted much more flexibility in the form of time-off and normal hours, because the company does not want to lose them. High performance is not a license to be smug around the office; to constantly march into your boss's office and make demands; or flaunt special arrangements with co-workers who don't have the same perks. But if you make an indispensable contribution to your Team Pulse and your company's strategic direction, you will be in a much better position to adapt your job to your personal direction. (If you need help determining how to do this, go back to chapter three and find the Team Pulse for your Team of One.)

The point is this: Pursuing excellence in your life does not have to conflict with the pursuit of excellence at work. In fact, just the opposite is often true. Pursuing excellence in your work can and should enhance your pursuit of personal excellence.

3. Quittin' Time

I mentioned earlier that the typical American makes 70 decisions every day. Think about that. That means you have 70 opportunities every day to either move yourself toward your chosen personal direction, or away from it. Decisions about what to eat, when to sleep, whether or not to exercise, how to prioritize your work projects and your home responsibilities, as well as which books to read, which people to spend your free time with, all play some role in supporting or hindering your personal strategy. As a result of reading this book, you should not only see your decisions in a new light. I hope you actually start to make decisions in a more strategic way. I hope you see that many of the most powerful decisions you can make—the decisions that will have the biggest impact on your success and happiness—are precisely the decisions that might feel the most painful in the moment. They are the decisions that will require you to let some trees burn in order to help your forest flourish.

But I also hope you see your surroundings differently. In the course of reading this book, I hope some of your epiphanies involved seeing opportunities for excellence in your life, your career, your organization, and your community that you might have missed up until now because they were covered in a thicket of lesser opportunities. Now, you know those opportunities exist. The next step is taking clear, decisive action to go get them. The only question left is: *What are you going to quit first?*

APPENDIX

If Your Decision Pulse Is...	Then Your Best Decisions...	And You Find Yourself Saying...	Famous People with this Decision Pulse
Authority	Reflect self-discipline and bring pride to your team, organization or family.	"My team respects authority. In order to keep the team functioning properly, people need to exercise self-discipline and respect the chain of command." "I send my children to private school. I don't like the expense, but I want my kids to have the structure a private school provides." "I declined a job offer because the people were too irreverent. Even though it was the kind of work I was looking for, I knew the people would annoy me sooner or later."	General George Patton Colin Powell Queen Elizabeth
Security	Provide safety and comfort for yourself and those you care about.	"The key players on my team have been the same for years. When I got promoted, I brought them with me. I knew I could count on them." "I send my kids to the school nearest our home. It has a decent reputation and I know my children will be safe walking there every day." "I took a new job because my last one was too unpredictable. Now I'm much more secure. The hours and expectations are more stable."	Warren Buffett Franklin D. Roosevelt

If Your Decision Pulse Is...	Then Your Best Decisions...	And You Find Yourself Saying...	Famous People with this Decision Pulse
Humanity	Help you contribute to society and make the world a better place.	"Everyone on my team is committed to social responsibility. If they don't have a strong moral compass, they aren't going to fit." "I send my kids to a public school. I want them to be exposed to many cultures, and I want to help maintain the quality of our local schools." "I took my current job because the company has a strong reputation for social responsibility. I know that my work makes the world a better place."	Mother Theresa Margaret Mead Ghandi
Relationships	Develop strong, close relationships with the people around you.	"My team is cohesive. I get to each person personally and professionally. We function more like a family than a work group." "I send my kids to the same school my friends' kids go to. Our friends really like the school, and it gives us a chance to strengthen our relationship." "I was going to quit, but then the company started a mentorship program. I got to know the people I work with much better. And I stayed."	Katherine Graham Bill Clinton Paul Revere

If Your Decision Pulse Is...	Then Your Best Decisions...	And You Find Yourself Saying...	Famous People with this Decision Pulse
Achievement	Push you toward important, long-term goals for your life and career.	"I assign clear, measurable objectives. To stay motivated, we have to track our progress. It can be difficult, but it always pays off in the end." "My kids go to the best school in the area. We decided to live here because of the educational experience and the opportunities the school provides." "I took this job because the compensation was too good to pass up. It was a good career move, with many opportunities for advancement."	Michael Phelps John Grisham Hillary Clinton
Power	Bring you greater influence, access and social standing.	"I thrive when my group looks to me for guidance. I do my best work and provide the most value when I can exercise that kind of influence." "I send kids to one of the most prestigious private schools in the city. The most powerful politicians and executives send their kids there too." "My job has unlimited opportunity for advancement. This company is one of the biggest names in the industry, and it commands a lot of respect."	Ronald Regan Oprah Winfrey Theodore Roosevelt

Stimulation	Maximize fun and adventure and keep life lively and interesting.	"I like to give my team exciting work. It might be a project that isn't well-defined, or one other teams believe is too risky. It keeps our work lively." "I send my kids to German immersion school. I thought it would be cool for my kids to have a different experience than I did." "I recently changed jobs again. The last one was exciting for a while, but it became too routine. I needed a bigger, bolder challenge."	Angelina Jolie Richard Branson Mick Jagger
Freedom	Remain independent and pursue new opportunities as they arise.	"I give my team total autonomy. Nobody likes to be micromanaged, and hand-holding eats up too much of my free time and creative energy." "I home-schooled my kids for a year while we traveled as a family. Some of my friends thought I was crazy, but it was incredibly liberating." "I'm an entrepreneur at heart. In my job, I'm free to do what I want, when I want. I don't know what the future holds, and that's all part of the fun."	Brenda Barnes Henry David Thoreau Matthew McConaughey

CPSIA information can be obtained at www.ICGtesting.com
Printed in the USA
BVOW07*0910051113

335274BV00002B/37/P